KITSCHY CRAFTS

JO PACKHAM & MATT SHAY

KITSCHY CRAFTS

A Celebration of Overlooked 20th Century Crafts

Jo Packham & Matt Shay

Sterling Publishing Co., Inc. New York

A Sterling/Chapelle Book

If you have any questions or comments, please contact:

Chapelle, Ltd.

P.O. Box 9252, Ogden, UT 84409

(801) 621-2777 • (801) 621-2788 Fax

e-mail: chapelle@chapelleltd.com

Web site: www.chapelleltd.com

The copy, photographs, and designs in this volume are intended for the personal use of the reader and may be reproduced for that purpose only. Any other use, especially commercial use, is forbidden under law without the written permission of the copyright holder.

Every effort has been made to ensure that all information in this book is accurate. However, due to differing conditions, tools, and individual skills, the publisher cannot be responsible for any injuries, losses, and/or other damages, which may result from the use of the information in this book.

This volume is meant to stimulate decorating ideas. If readers are not proficient in a skill necessary to attempt a project, we urge them to refer to an instructional book that addresses the required technique specifically.

Library of Congress Cataloging-in-Publication Data

Packham, Jo.

Kitschy crafts : a celebration of overlooked 20th century crafts / Jo Packham & Matt Shay.

p. cm.

Includes index.

"A Sterling/Chapelle Book."

ISBN 1-4027-1754-7

1. Handicraft. 2. Kitsch--United States--20th century. I. Shay, Matt. II. Title.

TT157.P223 2006

745.5--dc22

2005024041

10 9 8 7 6 5 4 3 2 1

Published by Sterling Publishing Co., Inc.

387 Park Ave. South, New York, NY 10016

©2006 by Jo Packham and Matt Shay

Distributed in Canada by Sterling Publishing

c/o Canadian Manda Group, 165 Dufferin St.

Toronto, Ontario, Canada M6K 3H6

Distributed in the United Kingdom by GMC Distribution Services,

Castle Place, 166 High Street, Lewes, East Sussex, England BN7 1XU

Distributed in Australia by Capricorn Link (Australia) Pty. Ltd.

P. O. Box 704, Windsor, NSW 2756, Australia

Printed and Bound in China

Sterling ISBN-13: 978-1-4027-1754-3

ISBN-10: 1-4027-1754-7

INVITATION TO *Smart Living*
THROUGH CRAFTING

Does your home décor have you stuck in Dullsville? Can't remember the last time you found crafting *fun*? Help is here . . . it's *Kitschy Crafts*.

That's right. *Kitschy Crafts*. Our top quality crafts will dazzle hubby, delight the kids, amaze your friends, and drive envy into the heart of every neighbor on your block.

And that's not all!

You'll find inspiration on every page of this volume. You'll see crafts you had forgotten and—we're willing to bet—crafts you never knew *could* exist.

For the fun of it, we've included instructions to help you achieve your own versions of some of the projects featured here.

Just try not to take any of it too seriously. After all, when you're crafting your way to a better life, it's a good idea to keep your sense of humor.

The fun way to get around!

Table of Contents

It's an all-star lineup

But, what is… Kitsch?

Once used to put down lowbrow art, the term "kitsch" has evolved to refer to any decoration that takes itself far too seriously. Ornamental statuary, knickknacks, souvenirs, and other simple decorative objects that are elevated to the role of sophisticated artwork are considered "kitschy." Author Sam Binkley observes, "As societies industrialized and more and more people gained access to mass-produced cultural goods, kitsch emerged as the lowest common cultural denominator of modern society, cutting across old class distinctions through the techniques of the new mass consumption."

The beauty of kitsch is that many of us feel an affection for that "lowest common denominator." A gentle smile crosses our faces when we tap the head of a bobble-headed sheep or lift a crocheted doll skirt to find a roll of toilet paper. When kitsch goes retro, it becomes a playful way to travel back in time and rediscover decorative techniques to bring into the present.

Baby boomers (those born between 1946 and 1964) have shaped cultural changes and caused social revolutions simply by growing up. As they reached high school and then college, their vast social voice gave rise to the beat generation of the 1950s—the antiwar movement, civil rights, women's liberation, and the hippie movement, just to name a few. Out of a disillusionment of industrialization and mass culture, they started a "back to the earth" philosophy of making your own way in the world that included making anything and everything by hand.

Now, those items born of social conscience are finding their way back into homes as hot collectibles. As the children of baby boomers grow up, there is a new fascination with the crafts of their parents' generation. So whether you want to take a trip down memory lane, have a bit of time on your newly retired hands, or are a young crafter wanting to try "new" things, open your mind and heart to a little bit of kitsch.

FADS • FADS • FADS

Fads of the 1950s
- Ant farms
- Blackjack chewing gum
- Bubble gum cigars
- Boomerangs
- Carhops
- Coonskin caps
- Frisbees
- Letter sweaters
- Panty raids
- Poodle skirts
- Saddle shoes
- Sideburns
- 3-D movies
- Virgin pins

Fads of the 1960s
- Bellbottoms
- Black lights
- Go-go boots
- Granny dresses
- Lava lamps
- Love beads
- Miniskirts
- Mood rings
- Rickie Tickie stickers
- Smiley faces
- Surfing
- The Twist
- Tie-dye
- Troll dolls

Fads of the 1970s
- Acupuncture
- Dashboard hula girls
- Disco
- Earth shoes
- 8-track tape players
- EST therapy
- Mexican jumping beans
- Mopeds
- Pet rocks
- Platform shoes
- Puka shells
- Star Wars action figures
- Streakers
- Video games

GREAT NEW KITCHEN IDEA!

the Decorator Refrigerator

"Now that's a kitschy kitchen!"

If you plan to cover your fridge, go beyond the simple cabinet panel. Take your look to a whole new level of custom—and kitsch.

K
KITSCH · MAKES IT POSSIBLE

French Provincial

Hacienda

PICK A THEME FOR YOUR NEW KITSCHY KITCHEN

Scenic

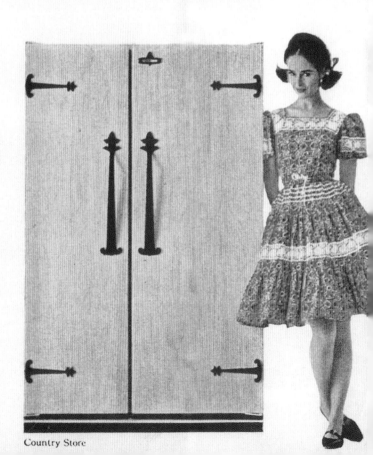

Country Store

Creative Rules of Thumb:

1. The best way to get great ideas is to get lots of ideas and throw the bad ones away.

2. Create ideas that are 15 minutes ahead of their time—not light-years ahead.

3. Always look for a second right answer.

4. If at first you don't succeed, take a break.

5. Write down your ideas before you forget them.

6. If everyone says you are wrong, you're one step ahead. If everyone laughs at you, you're two steps ahead.

7. The answer to your problem "preexists." You need to ask the right question to reveal the answer.

8. When you ask a dumb question, you get a smart answer.

9. Never solve a problem from its original perspective.

10. Visualize your problem as solved before solving it.

—Charles "Chic" Thompson

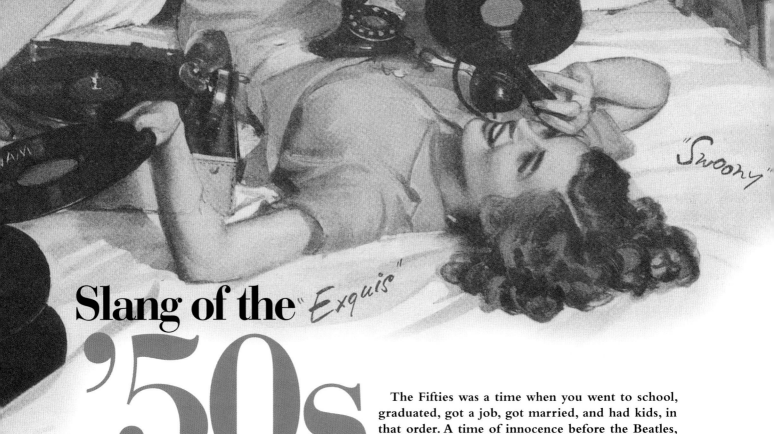

"Swoony"

Slang of the *"Exquis"* '50s

The Fifties was a time when you went to school, graduated, got a job, got married, and had kids, in that order. A time of innocence before the Beatles, hippies, or the Vietnam War. And like every generation, kids of the '50s had their own lingo.

Bad news: Depressing person

Bash: Great party

Blast: A good time

Boss: Great

Bread: Money

Bug: To bother

Cat: A hip person

Chariot: Car

Cherry: Anything really attractive

Cool: Extraordinary

Dig: To understand

Dolly: Cute girl

Earthbound: Reliable

Fake out: A bad date

Flick: A movie

Gig: Job

Hang: Hang out; do very little

Hep: With it; cool

Hip: In the know; very good

Jacketed: Going steady

Jets: Smarts; brains

Kick: Fun thing to do

Kookie: Nuts, in the nicest possible way

Later: Goodbye

Nod: Drift off to sleep

No sweat: No problem

Nowhere: Opposite of cool

Pad: Home

Party pooper: No fun at all

Passion pit: Drive-in movie theater

Peepers: Glasses

Rap: To tattle on someone

Rattle your cage: Get upset

Righto: Okay

Sides: Vinyl records

Sounds: Music

Split: Leave

Square: Conformist; normal person

The most: High praise

Threads: Clothes

Tight: Good friends

Unreal: Exceptional

13

The Sixties were fraught with social change—war, women's lib, civil rights. With this loss of innocence came a grittier lingo.

SLANG OF THE
1960s

A gas: A lot of fun

Bad: Awesome

Bag: To steal

Beat feet: Leave the scene in a hurry

Bitchin': Good; exciting; awesome

Blast: A great time

Blitzed: Intoxicated

Bogart: To "hog" something

Bookin': Going very fast, usually in a car

Boss: A great or cool thing

Bread: Money

Bug out: Leave the premises

Bummed out: Depressed

Cat: A guy

Chick: A girl or a woman

Choice: Really cool

Cool: Nice

Copasetic: Very good; all right

Crash: Go to bed; go to sleep

Decked out: Dressed up

Dig: Understand

Ditz: An idiot

Far out: Excellent; cool

Fink: A tattletale

Flake: A useless person

Flower child: A hippie

Freak out: Temporary loss of control due to an unpleasant event

Funky: Neat; cool. Also something gone bad, for example: I think that milk is funky.

Fuzz: The police

Hacked: Angry; disgusted

Hangin': Awesome; cool

Hang loose: Relax; take it easy

Heat: The police

Hip: Very good; cool

Jazzed: Elated; excited

Lay it on me: Speak your piece

Lip flappin': Talking about things of little importance

Loaded: Intoxicated

Old lady: Mother

Old man: Father

Outta sight: Fantastic; awesome

Pantywaist: A mama's boy; a geek

Peepers: Eyeglasses

Rags: Clothes

Right on: I agree; I concur

Righteous: Extremely fine; beautiful

Scratch: Money

Shades: Sunglasses

Solid: Something that is ok or all right

Tooling: To cruise or drive around without aim

Tough: Neat; cherry; great; bitchin'

Wicked: Term of admiration

Wiggin' out: Going crazy

Far out, man.

The edgy extremes of the Sixties evened out somewhat in the Seventies, leading to slang with a more laid-back feel.

Slang of the 1970's

A.F.A.: A friend always

Boss: Cool; awesome

Bread: Money; cash

Slanguage: The on-air language used over CB radios

Check ya later: See you later

Dy-no-mite: Great

Far out, man: Way cool

Foxy: Good looking

Gravy: Sweet; cool; excellent

Groovy: Cool

I hear that: I accept your decision

Jinkies: Exclamation of surprise

Jive turkey: A detestable person

Later: See you at another time

Let's book: Let's leave this place

Mellow out: Chill out; calm down

Outta sight: Very cool; good

Psychedelic: Awesome

Right on: Good; accepting something

See ya on the flipside: See you later

Solid: Cool

Streak: To run in public in the nude

Zoot: For something to go flailing outwards

Chapter 1

You know that needlework gives your clothing and home décor elegance and charm— but did you know that each stitch connects you to history? That's right! Ladies have been making statements with needle and thread for centuries. Mary, Queen of Scots, sewed secret messages in her creations and Betsy Ross stitched her name to the American Revolution with the first Stars and Stripes. Well-bred girls were long expected to fill their Hope Chests with embroidered linens, tablecloths, and other household items to share with their future husbands. The handiwork of the woman of the house was a symbol of status and good taste. So lift your needle proudly and join your sisters of the skein.

It's easier than fixing the evening meal!

"Me, needlework?" Of course you can! With so many homemakers relying on store-bought goods, just a few simple touches of embroidery make plain items luxurious and expensive-looking. (Only you need know how easy it is!)

And did you ever fancy yourself a rebel? Many in the Sixties believed that handcrafted clothing and decorations were a strike against the impersonal, mass-produced items that flooded their lives. The more society screamed for efficiency, the hungrier people were to express themselves through projects like those on the pages that follow.

NEEDLE nc CRAFTS

Needlework Primer

Definitions of a few types of needlework

Appliqué: Material is cut and sewn or fixed to a larger piece of fabric.

Assisi: Background is filled in with cross-stitches, leaving the design unstitched.

Bargello: Also called flame stitch or Hungarian point. Long vertical stitches worked on canvas, forming peaks or points. By varying colors, shaded effects are produced.

Blackwork: Geometric designs are stitched in black thread onto white or cream linen lengths. Backstitch, cross-stitch, and running stitch are used.

Canvaswork: Stitches of various length and slant cover an open-weave canvas. Also known as needlepoint in England.

Couching: Tiny stitches are used to hold one or more threads in position.

Counted Cross-stitch: A design is produced by counting and taking each stitch over a definite number of threads. Backstitch, cross-stitch, and four-sided, hem, and running stitches are used.

Cross-stitch: A finished design covering a premarked pattern on cloth with cross-stitches.

Crewel, or Jacobean, embroidery: Diverse stitches are worked in various wool yarns.

Cutwork: Parts of background are cut away and design is embroidered in the remaining blank space. Tiny running stitches are placed close to edge.

Drawn thread: Traditionally worked on fine linen, drawn thread is achieved through the contrast of open and closed areas created by removing threads from the fabric.

Hardanger: Combines satin stitches with drawn thread and cutwork.

Metal threadwork: The use of gold and metallic threads. Often threads are couched in place.

Needlepoint: Stitches of various length and slant cover an open-weave canvas.

Needleweaving: Threads are pulled from the fabric and replaced by weaving a design over and under the remaining threads.

Smocking: Small stitches used to anchor fabric that has been gathered into regular folds.

Stumpwork: Three-dimensional designs, or raised embroidery, achieved by placing batting between two layers of fabric, then stitching along the raised elements with silken threads.

Whitework: Stitches are worked with white threads on white fabric.

19

AHHH... APPLIQUÉ

Luxury. Nothing says it quite like appliqué. Whether applied to felt or cotton for wash-and-wear durability or stitched to gauze for delectable delicacy, this technique is the tasteful way to enhance your beds . . . your walls. . . your life.

Borrowed from quilters, appliqué gained popularity for its own sake in the 1970s. Modern crafters know its limitations are defined only by their own imaginations.

SIMPLE ENOUGH FOR A BEGINNER—YET INTRIGUING ENOUGH FOR THE MASTER!

Blue Appliqué

W A L L   H A N G I N G

The delicate beauty of this ballerina will dance straight
into your heart! Featherlight fabric is appliquéd to the
background to create a lovely wall hanging or bed cover.
(Tip: When working with sheer fabrics, baste rather than pin
the appliqué to the background to avoid puckering, and select
materials of comparable weight and texture.)

*Unparalleled
Beauty*

Sweet as a dream! Grace a lady's boudoir
with a dancer appliqué for wall or bedspread.

Diaphanous layers are stitched carefully to the background to ensure that this lovely lady stays put.
Hand-embroidered edging is the perfect finishing touch.

Wool Wall Hanging

A GROOVY ADDITION TO ANY ROOM

Graceful birds pose beneath a flowering tree in this wool wall hanging from the 1970s. To create this look, machine-stitch felt appliqué pieces to a wool background and embellish the design with embroidery. The heavyweight background holds up well against the thick thread. Staple the finished piece to stretcher bars for long-lasting protection.

Flowers were created with yarn and straight-stitch embroidery.

"I love what you've done"

and you will too with... Embroidery

From the rich robes of ancient kings to the airy peasant blouses favored by hippies of more recent years, embroidery has been making people's lives more beautiful for centuries. Though usually thought of as a decorative addition, embroidery can be functional as well, such as when used to secure contrasting pieces of cloth in appliqué.

For a time, pre-stamped designs were all the rage. While they remained popular through the 1960s, needleworkers of this time rediscovered the joy of inventing their own. Favoring white cotton and denim backgrounds, they used a dazzling array of stitches, including backstitch, buttonhole stitch, chain stitch, herringbone stitch, Lazy Daisy stitch, running stitch, satin stitch, and stem or outline stitch.

Days-of-the-Week Kitchen Towels
Kitchen towels go vintage with a variety of embroidery stitches.

Once used on flour-sack towels and other household items, simple embroidery continues to be popular with crafters and collectors. Traditionally, embroidery was stitched on plain cotton muslin. Although fabric choices abound today, most people still reach for cotton or linen in shades of white and ecru. Some even tea-stain fabric to make items look more authentic.

Tips for better embroidery stitching:

- Wash fabric prior to stitching.

- To prevent color from bleeding, soak thread in a mixture of vinegar and water prior to using. Allow thread to dry thoroughly.

- Use a split stitch or backstitch throughout entire project.

- Avoid designs with too much detail, as detail is lost when stitched in one color.

- Traditional themes include nursery rhymes, Sun Bonnet Sue, Bible stories, days of the week, and holiday designs.

Embroidery

Denim Shirts

Flowers bloom across a denim shirt, bringing feminine elegance to this Seventies-style denim work shirt.

Pillows

To create fabulous home fashions, combine embroidery with fabric paint. This pillow began with a design ironed onto plain fabric; the crafter then added paint and stitched the outlines before stuffing the pillow and sewing it closed.

Embroidery

CHIC & LOVELY

"North—South—East—West,
"Wherever you're cooking this
apron's the best"

The mark of the domestic queen is not a tiara—it's a fresh and pretty half-apron in pink gingham. Despite the delicate tulips and rickrack embellishment that set this project apart, you need not be needlework royalty to sew this project in a single afternoon.

Make this apron for use in your own kitchen or as a gift for your girlfriends.

28

Kitchen Half-apron
with embroidery

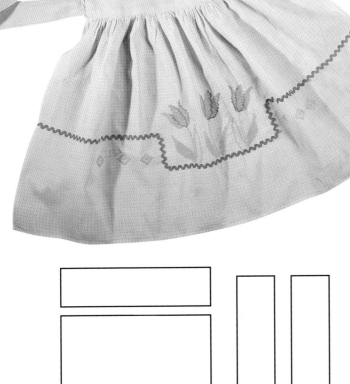

Materials

- Cotton fabric, 1 yard
- Sewing thread to match
- Embroidery thread
- Rickrack, 1 yard

Instructions

1. Cut fabric as shown in Diagram A.
2. Sew ¼" hem along top, bottom, and sides of large apron piece.
3. Fold in press ¼" seam allowance around all edges of waistband.
4. Sew a ¼" hem on long edges of ties and a 1" diagonal hem at one end of each tie.
5. Pleat remaining end of tie, fit into end of waistband, and stitch. Trim seam allowance, turn, and press.
6. Gather top of apron, and attach waistband.
7. Sew rickrack to front of apron.
8. Transfer any embroidery pattern or draw your own onto any apron and complete the embroidery with desired stitches.

Diagram A
⅒ scale

Are you a needlework newcomer? Fool your friends and neighbors! This smart apron requires easy-to-learn stitch techniques and the sewing is a snap—yet the results are so pretty, everyone will wonder, just how do you do it?

EXTRA! EXTRA!

If you can learn how to drive, you can learn to embroider.

When prepared canvas backing became widely available in the Seventies, droves of traditional weavers abandoned their cumbersome looms for latch hooking. The craze spread, and soon latch hooking was the yarn craft of choice for the average American family. While kits offer a fabulous introduction to this simplified form of weaving, creating designs of your own takes nothing more than a pencil, some graph paper, and a little imagination. (Pssst. For best results, keep designs simple!)

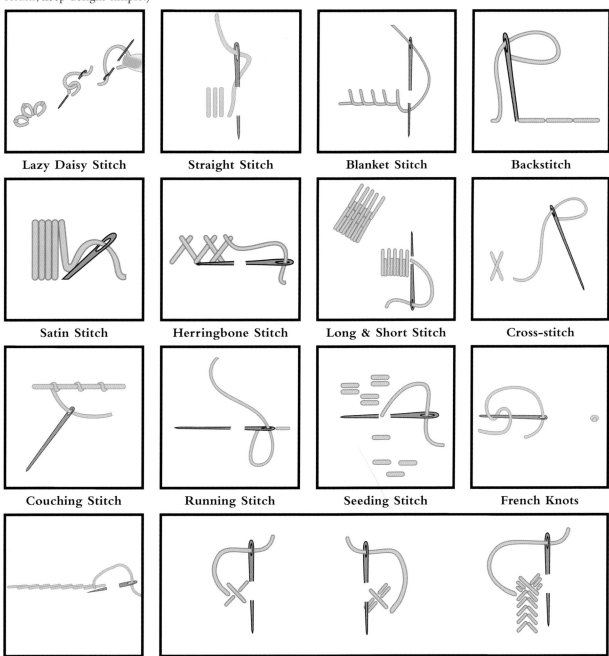

Lazy Daisy Stitch **Straight Stitch** **Blanket Stitch** **Backstitch**

Satin Stitch **Herringbone Stitch** **Long & Short Stitch** **Cross-stitch**

Couching Stitch **Running Stitch** **Seeding Stitch** **French Knots**

Outline Stitch **Close Herringbone Stitch**

Latch hooking is a simplified form of weaving. When prepared canvas backing became widely available in the 1970s, traditional weavers were eager to try the new craft. The absence of a cumbersome frame and the simplicity of methods used, made latch hooking the yarn craft of the average American family. Kits are a great way to introduce the techniques; but creating your own design takes only a bit of imagination, a pencil, and some graph paper. For guaranteed success, keep designs simple.

Latch-hook Wall Hanging

PRECUT PILE IS SIMPLY PULLED THROUGH THE CANVAS AND KNOTTED ON THE FRONT SIDE.

Materials

- Latch hook
- Yarn, available in skeins or in packages of 320 pre-cut pieces
- Canvas (For rectangular or square rugs, use canvas the exact width needed by 4" longer than needed. For round projects or cushions, use canvas 4" larger than the required diameter.)
- Rug binding tape
- Scissors

Instructions

Once you have decided on a design, work it out on paper first, then paint or draw onto canvas. Decide colors to use in each area of design. Draw your design on graph paper to scale so that each space represents one hole on the canvas.

To calculate the amount of yarn for each different color in your design, count the number of knots to be worked. When calculating the length of each strand, remember that each strand forms two lengths of pile and the knot uses up 1¼" of yarn. For a 2" length of pile, cut pieces 5¼" long. Count holes in each section of the design to determine how much of each color yarn is needed.

Basic Knots

Four-movement Knot

- Fold cut length of yarn in half then loop yarn around neck of hook below the crook and latch. Hold ends of yarn between the index finger and thumb of your least adept hand; insert hook under first of the weft threads. *Note: Weft threads are the threads running from left to right across the canvas.* Turn hook to the right, open the latch and place ends of yarn into hook. Pull hook under weft thread and through the loop of yarn. *Note: As you pull, the latch will close to prevent hook from getting caught in the canvas.*

Five-movement Knot

Use this knot when two people are working on a latch-hook piece from opposite ends. This ensures that pile will lie in the same direction.

- Insert hook under first weft thread. Fold cut length of yarn in half and, holding the ends between your thumb and index finger, loop yarn over hook. Pull hook back through canvas. Push hook through loop of yarn until latch is clear and loop is on neck of hook. Place cut ends of yarn into crook of hook from below, so ends are enclosed by latch. Pull hook back firmly through loop of yarn until ends are clear. Pull ends of yarn tightly to secure knot.

Prepare Piece for Hanging

- Fold top edge over and finish with binding tape, leaving sides of seam open. Insert drapery rod in pocket. Tie length of ribbon, tassel, or embellishment of your choice to ends of drapery rod as shown.

Nature themes were popular in the 1970s as they celebrated the earth and all of her gifts. The vintage mushroom forest rug was created from a kit. Kits continue to be widely popular and can be found in craft, sewing, and discount stores.

Chapter 2

__ Crochet __
THE ART OF HOOKING

Fine and lacy, thick and heavy—crochet stitches are as versatile as they are beautiful. There are many theories about the origins of crochet, but like all needlework arts, the historical facts are virtually impossible to pin down. This needlecraft came into vogue in the 1800s, and a variety of types developed, ranging from afghan to broomstick to Irish.

Through crochet, you can produce cozy afghans and warm sweaters to keep off the evening chill, elegant rosettes to warm the heart, innovative (and attractive!) kitchen solutions, and, of course, delicate doilies and darling dolls.

"I had no idea."

$\mathcal{B}$y the early 1900s, the Victorians (once again) drove the craft out of favor from sheer overindulgence, and crochet was not seen much until the 1950s. Still mostly a homemaker's craft, happy housewives created cozies, doilies, sweaters, pot holders, towels, and the ever popular afghan. In the 1960s, the younger population caught on and brought their own twist to the craft; a thicker yarn was used and bright colors were introduced. Everyone went crazy for crochet; new patterns and a free-spirited design was seen. Popular items to crochet included bright granny-square afghans, hats, scarves, and wall hangings. In the 1970s, crocheted clothing was all the rage. If one could wear it, someone somewhere tried a crochet version of it, from vests and skirts to bikinis and even bell bottoms. For the next few years, the interest in crochet waned; but now, once again, everyone seems to crochet, from moms to movie stars.

It's time to learn...

CROCHET A B C's

They're Easy!

alt	alternate	inc	increase
altog	altogether	incl	include(ing)
approx	approximately	in(s)	inch(es)
beg	begin(ning)	inst	instructions
bet	between	opp	opposite
BO	bind off	p	picot
ch	chain	patt	pattern
ch-1	chain previously made	pc	popcorn
cl	cluster	prec	preceding
cont	continue	rem	remain(ing)
CO	cast on	rep	repeat
col	color	rnd	round
cont	continue	sk	skip
dbl dec	double decrease	sl	slip
dble	double	sl st	slip stitch
dble tr	double-treble crochet	sm	small
dc	double crochet	sp	space
dec	decrease	st	stitch(es)
dec hdc	decrease half-double crochet	tog	together
diag	diagonal	tr	treble crochet
diam	diameter	tr tr	treble treble
dir	directions	v	v stitch
dk	dark	yo	yarn over
dtr	double treble	★	repeat all instructions between the asterisks
foll	following	()	repeat all instructions between the parentheses
htr	half treble	★	repeat to stopping point (e.g. repeat to ★)
hdc	half-double crochet		

37

Let's relax and get back to basics with…

Basic Crochet Stitches

- **Back post double crochet**: Yo, inset hook from to back between the posts of 1st and 2nd dc, then front again, between the posts of 2nd and 3rd dc. Yo, draw loop through twice.

- **Reverse sc**: Insert hook in st to the right. Yo, draw yarn through st. Yo draw yarn through 2 loops.

- **Chain stitch**: Yo, draw yarn through loop on hook, rep.

- **Double crochet**: Yo, inset hook in 5th chain from hook. Yo, draw yarn through st. Yo, draw yarn through 2 loops on hook. Yo, draw yarn through 2 loops on hook. Yo, inset hook in next st.

- **Double treble crochet**: Yo 3 times inset hook in 7th chain from hook. Yo, draw yarn through st, ★ Yo, draw yarn through 2 loops on hook ★ rep from ★ 3 times

- **Front Post double crochet**: Yo, inset hook from back to front between the posts of the 1st and 2nd dc, then to back again, between the posts of 2nd and 3rd dc. Yo, draw loop through twice.

- **Half double**: Yo, inset hook in 4th chain from hook. Yo, draw yarn through st, yo draw through 3 loops on hook.

- **Single crochet**: Inset hook in next ch from hook. Yo, draw yarn through st, yo draw yarn through 2 loops.

- **Slip stitch**: Inset hook in next st. Yo, draw yarn through st and loop on hook.

- **V stitch**: V stitch is a double crochet, chain stitch and double crochet in the same stitch

38

Afghan

It's more than luxurious comfort. It's more than a cheering splash of color. It's the must-have classic whenever cool winds blow and it's time to curl up in front of the hearth. It's an afghan.

The dramatic sweep of rich colors and textures fool many into believing they could never create an afghan as beautiful as their grandmother's. In truth, once you learn how to crochet a square in the pattern you desire, it is only a matter of patience, persistence, and consistency to produce elegant afghans for everyone you know.

For that extra touch, make rosettes separately, then stitch them to completed squares. Nothing could be easier!

Modern Living needs…

Rosettes

on your living room throw.

Chic décor calls for an elegant throw. Create your own cream-and-poppy beauty by adding rosettes to a plain background. Our instructions for making rosettes were inspired by this treasure from the Seventies.

Materials

- Perle cotton, size 5 (size 3 for a larger flower)
- Crochet hook, size 6/1.80mm (size D/3.325 for the size 3 cotton)
- Yarn needle

Single-color Rosette

Instructions

- Ch 17 (35, 53)
- **Row 1**: Dc in 5th ch from hook, ★ch 1, skip 1, (dc-ch-dc) in next ch =V-stitch made; repeat from ★ across; - 6 (16,25) V-stitches made. Turn.
- **Row 2**: Ch 3 –counts as dc, 5 dc in 1st ch space, ★sc in next ch-1 space, 6dc in next ch-1 space – shell st made; repeat from ★, ending 6dc in last ch-1 space- 6 (16,25) shells. Fasten off, leaving long tail for anchoring rosette.
- **Finishing:** Thread needle with tail and weave to base of last st. Starting at that end, roll first shell tightly to form center bud; anchor at base of shell with 2 sts. Roll remaining strip to form Rosette, then secure by stitching in and out through layers for foundation ch at bottom of Rosette. If you want to make your Rosette a pin or barrette, sew or glue pin back or barrette back to back of Rosette.

Two-color Rosette

Instructions

- Ch 17 (35,53)
- **Row 1**: Dc in 5th ch from hook, ★ch 1 skip 1, (dc-ch-dc) in next ch =V-stitch made; repeat from ★ across; -6 (16,25) V-stitches made. Turn.
- **Row 2**: Ch 3 – counts as dc, 5 dc in 1st ch- space, ★sc in next ch-1 space, 6 dc in next ch-1 space- shell st made; repeat from ★ ending 6 dc in last ch-1-space – 6 (16,25) shells. Fasten off, leaving long tail for anchoring rosette. Work last dc of last shell until 2 loops remain on hook, drop main color, finish st with new color, ch1, and turn.
- **Row 3**: sc in each st across. Fasten off.
- **Finishing**: Thread needle with tail and weave to base of last st. Starting at same end, roll 1st shell tightly to form center bud; anchor at base of shell with 2 sts. Roll remaining strip to form Rosette, then secure by stitching in and out through layers of foundation ch at bottom of Rosette.

"Dinner is a Snap with Funky Glass Jacks."

42

Funky Glass Jacks

"Bugs in my guest's lemonade? Circles on my coffee table? Never again!"

Also known as cup cozies, these hip beverage covers fit snugly over glasses to keep out pests. Slip one over the glass bottom for an attractive and practical coaster.

Only Quality Materials

- Crochet hook, size 6–8
- Crochet thread, size 10

INSTRUCTIONS

- **Ch 5**; join with a sl st in the 1st ch to form ring.

- **Rnd 1**: ch 3 to count as 1st dc, work 11 dc in the ring; join with sl st in top of beginning ch 3. (12 dc)

- **Rnd 2**: ch 3 to count as the 1st dc, dc in the same st as joining, work 2 dc in each remaining dc around; join with sl st in the top of the beginning ch 3. (24 dc)

- **Rnd 3**: ch 3 to count as 1st dc, 2 dc in next dc, (dc in next dc, 2 dc in the next dc) 11 times; join with sl st in top of the beginning ch 3. (36 dc)

- **Rnd 4**: ch 5 to count as 1st dc and 1st ch 2, work dc in the same st as joining, sk next 2 dc, ★(dc, ch 2, dc) in the next dc, sk next 2 dc ★ Repeat from ★ to ★ 9 times; join with sl st in the 3rd ch of the beginning ch 5. (12 V-sts)

- **Rnds 5–12**: sl st into 1st ch-2 sp, ch 5 to count as 1st dc, and the 1st ch 2, dc in same space, (dc, ch 2, dc) 11 times, ch-2 sps around; join with a sl st in 3rd ch of beginning ch 5. (12 V-sts)

- **Rnd 13**: sl st into first ch-2 sp, ch 5, hdc in 3rd ch from hook dc in the same space, (dc, ch 2) hdc in the top dc, dc in the same sp 11 times, ch-2 sps around; join with a sl st in the 3rd ch of beginning ch 5. (12 picot V-sts) Fasten off.

Styled by
PINWHEEL DOILY

The white-on-white color scheme fits perfectly with every family and their modern décor.

MATERIALS

- Crochet thread, 2 balls
- Steel crochet hook, size 8–9

INSTRUCTIONS

- Starting at center, ch 6, join with sl st to form ring.
- **Rnd 1**: ch 4, (dc in ring, ch 1) 11 times; join with sl st to 3rd st of 1st ch made (12 dc counting 1st ch as 1 dc).
- **Rnd 2**: sl st in next sp, ch 3, dc in same sp, ★ ch 2, 2 dc in next sp. Repeat from ★ around, joining last ch–2 to 3rd st of 1st ch made.
- **Rnd 3**: ch 3, dc in next dc, dc in next sp, ★ ch 2, dc in each of next 2 dc, dc in next sp. Repeat from ★ around. Join.
- **Rnd 4**: sl st in next dc, ch 3, 2 dc in next dc, dc in next sp, ★ ch 3, skip 1 dc, dc in next dc, 2 dc in next dc, dc in next sp. Repeat from ★ around. Join.
- **Rnd 5**: sl st in next dc, ch 3, dc in next dc, ★ 2 dc in next dc, dc in next sp, ch 3, skip 1 dc, dc in 2 dc. Repeat from ★ around. Join.

Delicate as a snowflake, yet warming to the heart, a pretty doily means even more when made by your own hands.

- **Rnd 6**: sl st in next dc, ch 3, dc in 2 dc, ★ 2 dc in next dc, dc in next sp, ch 3, skip 1 dc, dc in 3 dc. Repeat from ★ around. Join.

- **Rnds 7–12**: continue as above, but work 1 more dc in each group on each rnd until there are 12 dc in each group at end of 12th rnd. Join.

- **Rnd 13**: sl st in next dc, ch 3, dc in 10 dc, ★ ch 9, skip 1 dc, dc in 11 dc. Repeat from ★ around. Join.

- **Rnd 14**: sl st in next dc, ch 3, dc in 9 dc, ★ ch 5, sc in next loop, ch 3, sc in same loop, ch 5, skip 1 dc, dc in next 10 dc. Repeat from ★ around. Join.

- **Rnd 15**: sl st in next dc, ch 3, dc in 8 dc, ★ ch 5, sc in next ch-5 loop, ch 3, sc in next ch-3 loop, ch 3, sc in next ch-5 loop, ch 5, skip 1 dc, dc in 9 dc. Repeat from ★ around. Join.

- **Rnd 16**: sl st in next dc, ch 3, dc in 7 dc, ★ ch 5, sc in next loop, (ch 3, sc in next loop) 3 times; ch 5, skip 1 dc, dc in next 8 dc. Repeat from ★ around. Join.

- **Rnd 17**: sl st in next dc, ch 3, dc in 6 dc, ★ ch 5, sc in next loop, (ch 3, sc in next loop) 4 times; ch 5, skip 1 dc, dc in next 7 dc. Repeat from ★ around. Join.

- **Rnd 18**: sl st in next dc, ch 3, dc in 5 dc, ★ ch 11, skip 1 loop, sc in next loop, (ch 3, sc in next loop) 3 times; ch 11, skip 1 loop and 1 dc, dc in 6 dc. Repeat from ★ around. Join.

- **Rnd 19**: sl st in next dc, ch 3, dc in 4 dc, ★ ch 5, sc in next loop, ch 3, sc in same loop, ch 5, sc in next loop, (ch 3, sc in next loop) twice; ch 5, sc in next loop, ch 3, sc in same loop, ch 5, skip 1 dc, dc in 5 dc. Repeat from ★ around. Join.

- **Rnd 20**: sl st in next dc, ch 3, dc in 3 dc, ★ ch 5, sc in next loop, (ch 3, sc in next loop) twice; ch 5, sc in next loop, ch 3, sc in next loop, ch 5, sc in next loop, (ch 3, sc in next loop) twice; ch 5, skip 1 dc, dc in 4 dc. Repeat from ★ around. Join.

- **Rnd 21**: sl st in next dc, ch 3, dc in 2 dc, ★ ch 5, sc in next loop, (ch 3, sc in next loop) 3 times; ch 11, sc in next loop, (ch 3, sc in next loop) 3 times; ch 5, skip 1 dc, dc in 3 dc. Repeat from ★ around. Join.

- **Rnd 22**: sl st in next dc, ch 3, dc in next dc, ★ ch 7, skip 1 loop, sc in next loop, (ch 3, sc in next loop) twice; ch 7, dc in next loop, ch 7, sc in next loop, (ch 3, sc in next loop) twice; ch 7, skip 1 loop and 1 dc, dc in 2 dc. Repeat from ★ around. Join and turn.

DOILY
the Possibilities are endless.

- **Rnd 23**: sl st in last loop, ch 6, turn, dc in next loop, ★ ch 8, sc in next loop, ch 3, sc in next loop, ch 8, dc in next loop, ch 3, dc in next loop. Repeat from ★ around. Join to 3rd st of turning ch.

- **Rnd 24**: sl st in next sp, ch 6, dc in next sp, ★ ch 15, dc in next ch-8 loop, ch 3, dc in next ch-3 sp, ch 3, dc in next loop. Repeat from ★ around. Join.

- **Rnd 25**: sl st in next sp, ch 10, ★ dc in next loop, ch 3, dc in same loop, ch 7, dc in next sp, ch 3, dc in next sp, ch 7. Repeat from ★ around. Join.

- **Rnd 26**: sl st across 7 ch, ch 6, dc in next sp, ★ ch 3, dc in next loop, ch 17, dc in next ch-7 loop, ch 3, dc in next sp. Repeat from ★ around. Join.

- **Rnd 27**: sl st in next sp, ch 6, dc in next sp, ★ ch 8, in next loop make dc, ch 3, and dc, ch 8, dc in next sp, ch 3, dc in next sp. Repeat from ★ around. Join.

- **Rnd 28**: sl st across 3 ch, 1 dc and 7 ch, ch 6, dc in next sp, ch 3, dc in next loop, ★ ch 11, dc in next ch-8 loop, ch 3, dc in next sp, ch 3, dc in next loop. Repeat from ★ around. Join.

- **Rnd 29**: ch 3, 3 dc in each of next 2 sps, dc in next dc, ★ ch 2, 8 dc in next loop, ch 2, dc in next dc, 3 dc in each of next 2 sps, dc in next dc. Repeat from ★ around. Join.

- **Rnd 30**: sl st in next dc, ch 3, dc in 6 dc, ★ ch 4, skip 1 dc, dc in 7 dc. Repeat from ★ around. Join.

- **Rnd 31**: sl st in next dc, ch 3, dc in 5 dc, ★ ch 6, skip 1 dc, dc in 6 dc. Repeat from ★ around. Join.

- **Rnd 32**: sl st in next dc, ch 3, dc in 4 dc, ★ ch 7, skip 1 dc, dc in 5 dc. Repeat from ★ around. Join.

- **Rnd 33**: sl st in next dc, ch 3, dc in 3 dc, ★ ch 9, skip 1 dc, dc in 4 dc. Repeat from ★ around. Join.

- **Rnd 34**: sl st in next dc, ch 3, dc in 2 dc, ★ ch 10, skip 1 dc, dc in 3 dc. Repeat from ★ around. Join.

- **Rnd 35**: sl st in next dc, ch 3, dc in next dc, ★ ch 12, skip 1 dc, dc in next 2 dc. Repeat from ★ around. Join.

- **Rnd 36**: sl st in next dc, ch 17, ★ skip 1 dc, dc in next dc, ch 14. Repeat from ★ around. Join and fasten off.

Styled by PINWHEEL DOILY

Intricate detail . . . timeless beauty. It can be yours with the dazzling pinwheel doily.

46

"It's just the open road
. . . and a doily . . . for me!"

Smart, darling doilies make everything nicer. From the table to the collar of your favorite motoring suit, a doily brings feminine flair to whatever it touches. Stitched or pinned into place, it becomes "wearable art."

"I turned my doily into wearable art!"

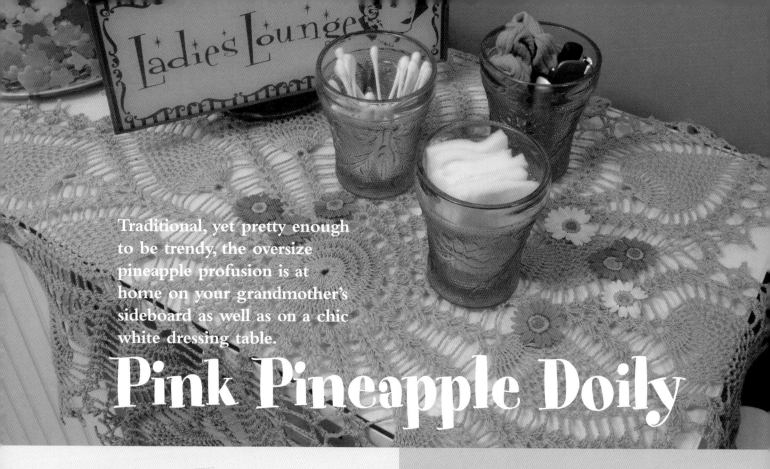

Traditional, yet pretty enough to be trendy, the oversize pineapple profusion is at home on your grandmother's sideboard as well as on a chic white dressing table.

Pink Pineapple Doily

Materials

- Yarn, 2-ply cotton, 3 balls
- Steel crochet hook, size 12

Instructions

- Starting at center, ch 16, join with sl st
- **Rnd 1**: ch 3, 32 dc in ring, sl st in 3rd st of ch-3.
- **Rnd 2**: ch 3, dc in each dc around; join to 3rd st of ch-3.
- **Rnd 3**: Ch 3, dc in same place as 51st, 2 dc in each dc around, sl st in 3rd st of ch-3.
- **Rnd 4**: Repeat 2nd rnd.
- **Rnd 5**: Ch 3, dc in same place as 51st, ★ ch 3, skip 2 dc, 2 dc in next dc. Repeat from ★ around, ending with ch 3, join to 3rd st of ch-3 (22 dc).
- **Rnd 6**: sl st in next dc and in next sp, ch 3; in same sp make dc, ch 2 and 2 dc; in each ch-3 sp around make 2 dc, ch 2 and 2 dc. Join.
- **Rnd 7**: sl st in next dc and in next ch 2 sp, ch 3, in same sp make dc, ch 2 and 2 dc; ★ ch 1, in next ch-2 sp make 2 dc, ch 2 and 2 dc (shell over shell). Repeat from ★ around, ending with ch-1. Join.

- **Rnds 8-12**: Repeat 7th rnd, having an extra ch between each shell in each rnd.
- **Rnd 13**: sl st in next dc and in next sp, ch 3; in same sp make dc, ch 5 and 2 dc . ★ Ch 6, in next ch-2 sp make 2 dc, ch 2 and 2 dc, ch 6; in next ch-2 sp make 2 dc, ch 5 and 2 dc. Repeat from ★ around. Join.
- **Rnd 14**: sl st in next dc and in next sp, ch 4, 12 tr in ch-5 of shell, ★ ch 5, in next ch-2 make 2 dc, ch 2 and 2 dc; ch 5, 13 tr in ch-5 of next shell. Repeat from ★ around, ending with ch 5. Join.
- **Rnd 15**: ch 5 (to count as tr and c h-1), tr in next tr; (ch 1, tr in next tr) 11 times; ★ ch 3, shell over next shell, ch 3, tr in next tr; (ch 1, tr in next tr) 12 times. Repeat from ★ around; join to 4th st of ch-5 first made.
- **Rnd 16**: sl st in 1st ch-1 sp, sc in same sp; ★ (ch 3, sc in next ch-1 sp) 11 times, ch 3, shell over next shell, ch 3, sc in next ch-1 sp. Repeat from ★ around, ending with ch 3, sc in 1st ch-3 loop.
- **Rnd 17**: (ch 3, sc in next loop) 10 times, ★ ch 3, shell over next shell; (ch 3, sc in next loop) 11 times. Repeat from ★ around, ending with ch 3, sc in 1st ch-3 loop.
- **Rnd 18**: (ch 3, sc in next loop) 9 times, ★ ch 3, in ch-2 of next shell make 2 dc, ch 2, 2 dc, ch 2 and 2 dc. (ch 3, sc in next loop) 10 times. Repeat from ★ around, ending with ch 3, sc in 1st ch-3 loop.

- **Rnd 19**: (ch 3, sc in next loop) 8 times, ★ ch 3, in next ch-2 make a shell around, ending with ch 3, sc in 1st ch-3 loop.
- **Rnd 20**: (ch 3, sc in next loop) 7 times, ★ ch 5, shell over next shell, ch 1, shell in next ch-2 sp, ch 1, shell over next shell; (ch 3, sc in next loop) 8 times. Repeat from ★ around, ending with ch 3, sc in 1st ch-3 loop.
- **Rnd 21**: (ch 3, sc in next loop) 6 times; ★ (ch 3, shell over next shell) 3 times; (ch 3, sc in next loop) 7 times. Repeat from ★ around, ending with ch 3, sc in 1st ch-3 loop.
- **Rnd 22**: (ch 3, sc in next loop) 5 times, ★ ch 3, shell over next shell; (ch 4, shell over next shell) twice; (ch 3, sc in next loop) 6 times. Repeat from ★ around.
- **Rnd 23**: (ch 3, sc in next loop) 4 times; ★ ch 3, shell over next shell, ch 5; in next shell make 2 dc, ch 5 and 2 dc; ch 5, shell over next shell; (ch 3, sc in next loop) 5 times. Repeat from ★ around.
- **Rnd 24**: (ch 3, sc in next loop) 3 times; ★ ch 3, shell over next shell, ch 3, 14 tr in next shell, ch 3, shell over next shell; (ch 3, sc in next loop) 4 times. Repeat from ★ around.
- **Rnd 25**: (ch 3, sc in next loop) twice; ★ ch 3, shell over next shell, ch 3, tr in next tr; (ch 1, tr in next tr) 13 times; ch 3, shell over next shell; (ch 3, sc in next loop) 3 times. Repeat from ★ around.
- **Rnd 26**: ch 3, sc in next loop, ★ ch 3, shell over next shell; (ch 3, sc in next ch-1 sp) 13 times; ch 3, shell over next shell; (ch 3, sc in next loop) twice. Repeat from ★ around.
- **Rnd 27**: ★ ch 4, shell over next shell; (ch 3, sc in next loop) 12 times; ch 3, shell over next shell; ch 4, sc in next loop. Repeat from ★ around, ending with ch 4, sl st in 1st sc. Fasten off.
- **Rnd 28**: ★ attach thread to ch-2 of next shell of previous rnd, ch 3; make dc, ch 2 and 2 dc in same shell; (ch 3, sc in next loop) 11 times; ch 3, shell over next shell. ch 3, turn.
- **Rnds 29-36**: Shell over shell; (ch 3, sc in next loop) 10 times; ch 3, shell over next shell; ch 3, turn. Continue in this manner, making 1 ch-3 loop less on each row until 36th row is completed.
- **Rnd 37**: Shell over shell; (ch 3, sc in next loop) twice; ch 3, shell over shell- 1 loop remaining at point. ch 3, turn. Make shell over shell, ch 4, sc in next loop, ch 4, 2 dc in next shell, ch 1, sl st back in ch-2 of last shell; ch 1, 2 dc where last 2 dc were made. Fasten off. Attach thread to ch-2 of next shell of 27th rnd and complete the next point in same manner. Continue until all 11 points have been worked; then work edging:

Edging:

- **Rnd 1**: attach thread to tip of one point where shells were joined, ch 3, in same place where ch-3 was joined make dc, ch 2 and 2 dc. ★ (ch 3, shell in next turning ch, between 2 rows) 5 times; ch 2, dc in ch-2 of shell preceding ch-4 (on 27th rnd), holding back the last loop of this dc and next dc on hook; dc in ch-2 of next shell (where thread was attached, to work point); thread over and draw through all loops on hook; (ch 3, shell in turning ch between 2 rows) 5 times; ch 3, shell at tip of next point, where shells were joined. Repeat from ★ around. Join last ch-3 to 3rd st of ch-3.
- **Rnd 2**: sl st in next dc and in next sp, ch 8, sc in 5th ch from hook . dc in same place as sl st, ★ ch 3, sc under next ch-3, ch 3; in next shell make dc, p and dc. Repeat from ★ 4 more times, ch 3, sc in next dc, ch 3; in next shell make dc, p and dc. ch 3, sc under next ch-3. Repeat all the way around. Fasten off.

GRAPE DOILY

Place this lovely item beneath a bottle of wine for a graciously set table your friends will admire.

MATERIALS
• Crochet yarns: green, 1 ball; purple, 2 balls; white, 1 ball, 2 ply cotton
• Crochet hook, size 7

50

WHITE

- Starting at center with white yarn, ch 10. Join with sl st to form ring.
- **Rnd 1**: ch 5, (dc in ring, ch 2) 15 times; join to 3rd ch of ch-5 (16 sps).
- **Rnd 2**: sl st in next sp, ch 3, dc in same sp, ★ ch 2, 2 dc in next sp. Repeat from ★ around. Join last ch-2 to top of ch-3.
- **Rnd 3**: sl st in next sp, ch 3, in same sp make dc, ch 3 and 2 dc; ★ in next sp make 2 dc, ch 3 and 2 dc (shell made). Repeat from ★ around. Join.
- **Rnds 4–5**: sl st to sp of next shell, ch 3, in same shell make 2 dc, ch 3 and 3 dc; ★ in sp of next shell make 3 dc, ch 3 and 3 dc. Repeat from ★ around. Join.
- **Rnds 6–7**: sl st to sp of next shell, ch 3, in same shell make 3 dc, ch 3 and 4 dc; ★ in next sp make 4 dc, ch 3 and 4 dc. Repeat from ★ around. Join.
- **Rnd 8**: sl st to sp of next shell, ch 3, in same shell make 3 dc, ch 3 and 4 dc; ★ ch 2, dc in first dc of next shell, ch 2, in sp of next shell make 4 dc, ch 3 and 4 dc. Repeat from ★ around. Join.
- **Rnd 9**: sl st to sp of next shell, ch 3, in same sp make 4 dc, ch 3 and 5 dc; ★ ch 2, skip next sp, dc in next dc, ch 2, in sp of next shell make 5 dc, ch 3 and 5 dc. Repeat from ★ around. Join and break off.
- **Rnd 10**: attach green yarn to sp of any shell, ch 4, in same sp make 4 tr, ch 3 and 5 tr; ★ ch 5, in sp of next shell make (tr, ch 2) 9 times and tr (9 sps); ch 5, in sp of next shell make 5 dc, ch 3 and 5 dc. Repeat from ★ around. Join and break off.

GRAPES

- **Row 1**: Attach purple yarn to first sp of any 9-sp group, ch 3, in same sp make 9 dc, drop loop from hook, insert hook in top of first st of this group, draw dropped loop through (pc st made); ★ ch 2, make 10 dc in next sp, insert hook in first dc of group and complete pc st. Repeat from ★ across remaining 7 sps. ch 3, turn.
- **Row 2**: 9 dc in first ch-2 sp, drop loop from hook, insert hook in top of ch-3 from back to front, draw dropped loop through (inverted pc st); ★ ch 2, 10 dc in next sp, complete an inverted pc s1. Repeat from ★ across each remaining sp. Ch 3, turn (8 pc sts).
- Continue working rows of pc sts, having 1 less pc st on each row, until 1 pc st remains. Break off.
- Repeat above steps to make a bunch of grapes over each group of sps.

Deep purple grapes are stunning when set against a dark green background.

GREEN

- **Row 1**: Attach green yarn to tip of last pc st made on first row of any set of grapes, ch 5, in sp of shell make 4 tr, ch 3 and 4 tr, (shell made); ch 5, sl st in tip of first pc st on first row of next set of grapes, ch 3, sl st in tip of pc st on next row, ch 5, turn.
- **Rows 2–3**: Make shell in sp of shell, ch 5, sl st in tip of pc st on next row of grapes, ch 3, sl st in tip of pc st on following row. ch 5, turn.
- **Row 4**: 4 tr in sp of shell, ch 3, in same sp make (3 tr, ch 3) twice and 4 tr; ch 5, sl st in tip of next pc st, ch 3, sl st in tip of pc st on next row. ch 5, turn.
- **Row 5**: Shell in sp of first shell, ch 3, sc in next sp, ch 3, shell in next sp, ch 5, sl st in tip of next pc st, ch 3, sl st in tip of pc st on next row. Ch 5, turn.
- **Row 6**: Shell in first shell, (ch 3, sc in next sp) twice; ch 3, shell in sp of next shell, ch 5, sl st in tip of next pc st, ch 3, sl st in tip of pc st on next row. ch 5, turn.
- **Row 7**: Shell in sp of next shell, ch 3, sc in next sp, ch 3, shell in next loop, ch 3, sc in next sp, ch 3, shell in sp of next shell, ch 5, sl st in tip of next pc st, ch 3, sl st in tip of pc st on next row. ch 5, turn.
- **Row 8**: Shell in sp of next shell, (ch 3, sc in next sp) twice; ch 3, shell in sp of next shell, (ch 3, sc in next sp) twice; ch 3, shell in sp of next shell, ch 5, sl st in tip of next pc st, ch 3, sl st in tip of pc st on next row. ch 5, turn.
- **Row 9**: ★ tr in sp of next shell, ch 3, sl st in tr just made (picot made), in same sp make (2 tr, picot) 4 times; (ch 3, sc in next sp, picot) 3 times; ch 3. Repeat from ★ once more; in next sp make tr, picot, (2 tr, picot) 4 times; ch 5, sl st in tip of top pc st. Break off.
- Repeat above steps to work remaining leaves.
- Starch lightly and press.

Your new countertops are safe with...

Hubby and kids see stylish, attractive trivets. The Mrs. knows her counters will stay beautiful.

Bottle-cap Trivets

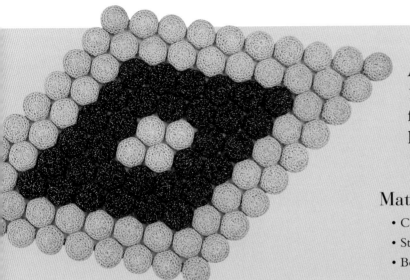

A favorite kitchen project from the 1950s, bottle-cap trivets are perfect for use in retro kitchens, country kitchens, or just really busy kitchens.

Metallic thread lends an elegant look to this diamond-shaped bottle-cap trivet.

Materials

- Cotton thread, size 10
- Steel crochet hook, size #7
- Bottle caps.

Instructions

- Starting at center, ch 4.
- **Rnd 1**: 19 dc in 4th ch from hook. Join to top of ch-4.
- **Rnd 2**: 2 sc in same place as sl st, ★ sc in next 4 dc, 2 sc in next dc. Repeat from ★ around. Join.
- **Rnds 3–6**: Sc in each sc around. Join.
- **7th rnd**: Ch 3, dc in each sc around. Join and break off, leaving a 6" length of thread. Insert bottle cap and sew up opening by gathering last rnd.
- **Finishing**: When all bottle caps are covered, sew together in desired pattern, using a whipstitch on back side. Secure all knots.

Also Available in Fancy Fruit Styles

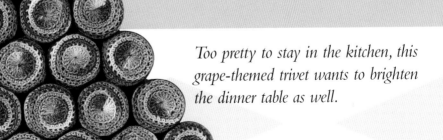

Too pretty to stay in the kitchen, this grape-themed trivet wants to brighten the dinner table as well.

"*Hey, don't forget your Fancy Pants Dishcloth!*"

Fancy Pants Dishcloth

A delight to find on flea market excursions, dishcloth bloomers also make a terrific gift.

The dishcloth bloomers make a wonderful house-warming gift. For added surprise, create the gift in the colors of the new home.

To use the dishcloth pants, all you have to do is untie the ribbon. They are so cute, you may want to make two pairs—one to save and one to use.

Materials

- 2 loosely woven dishcloths
- Crochet hook, size 5 or tapestry needle with large eye
- Ribbon in coordinating color, 1½ yards
- Straight pins

Instructions

1. Fold each dishcloth lengthwise and pin along the edges. Place the two dishcloths together with the side seams facing toward the center.

2. Use the crochet hook or embroidery needle to thread ribbon around the cuff of one pant leg. Begin at the center front of the leg so the loose ends of the ribbon meet there. Note: You will use about 12" of ribbon on each side. Pull the ribbon to create slight gathers and tie a bow. Repeat on the other side.

3. Attach the two pant legs to each other by weaving 18" of ribbon through the top of each dishcloth to create a "waistband." Again, tie a bow at the center front.

4. Join the sides of the pant legs by inserting an 18" ribbon under the bow at the waistband. Position the ribbon so that two equal lengths are on each side. Thread the ribbon down the dishcloths, using a crisscross pattern (like lacing a shoe). Two-thirds of the way down, tie the loose ends of the ribbon into a bow. Remove all pins.

Groovy Bed Doll

Materials

- 2 white buttons, medium
- 13" doll
- Crochet hook, size G
- Thin white ribbon, 2 yds
- Yarn, 3 ply: 3 orange; 2 white

Instructions

Bodice

- **Row 1**: with orange, ch 21, sc in 2nd ch from hook & in each ch across, ch 1, turn (20 sc).
- **Row 2**: ★ sc in next sc, 2 sc in next sc. Repeat from ★ across, ch 1, turn. (30 sc)
- **Row 3**: sc in each sc across, ch 1, turn. (30 sc)
- **Row 4**: ★ sc in next 2 sc, 2 sc in next sc. Repeat from ★ across, ch 1, turn. (40 sc)
- **Row 5**: sc in next 6 sc, ch 4, sk next 8 sc, sc in next 12 sc, ch 4, sk next 8 sc, sc in last 6 sc, ch 1, turn. (These are the armholes.)
- **Row 6**: sc in each sc and ch across, ch 1, turn. (32 sc)
- **Row 7**: sc in next 8 sc, dc over next 2 sc, sc in next 12 sc, dc over next 2 sc, sc in last 8 sc, ch 1, turn. (30 sc)
- **Rows 8–17**: sc in each sc across, ch 1, turn. (30 sc)
- **Row 18**: sc in each sc across, ch 3, turn. (30 sc)

Skirt

- **Row 19**: Working in bl opp, 3 dc in each sc across, join with sl st in top of beg ch 3, do not turn. ch 3 (does not count as dc). (90 dc) (From here onward, you will be working in Rnds.)
- **Rnds 20–21**: dc in each dc around, join, ch 3 (90 dc).
- **Rnd 22**: ★ dc in next 8 dc, 2 dc in next dc. Repeat from ★ around, join, ch 3 (100 dc)
- **Rnd 23**: working in bl opp, dc in each dc around, join, ch 3. (100 dc)
- **Rnd 24**: ★ dc in next 9 dc, 2 dc in next dc. Repeat from ★ around, join, ch 3 (110 dc)
- **Rnd 25**: Repeat Rnd 20. (110 dc)
- **Rnd 26**: ★ dc in next 10 dc, 2 dc in next dc. Repeat from ★ around, join, ch 3. (120 dc)
- **Rnd 27**: Repeat Rnd 23. (120 dc)

- **Rnd 28**: ★ dc in next 11 dc, 2 dc in next dc. Repeat from ★ around, join, ch 3. (130 dc)
- **Rnd 29**: Repeat Rnd 20. (130 dc)
- **Rnd 30**: ★ dc in next 12 dc, 2 dc in next dc. Repeat from ★ around, join, ch 3. (140 dc)
- **Rnd 31**: Repeat Rnd 20. (140 dc)
- **Rnd 32**: ★ dc in next 13 dc, 2 dc in next dc. Repeat from ★ around, join, ch 3. (150 dc)
- **Rnd 33**: Repeat Rnd 20. (150 dc)
- **Rnd 34**: ★ dc in next 14 dc, 2 dc in next dc. Repeat from ★ around, join. Fasten off orange. (160 dc)

Bottom Ruffle

- **Rnd 35**: Join white with sl st in first dc, ch 3, (dc, ch 2, 2 dc) in same sp, sk 2 dc, ★(2 dc, ch 2, 2 dc) in next dc, sk 2 dc. Repeat from ★ around, join with sl st in top of beginning ch 3 (54 shells).
- **Rnd 36**: sl st to ch 2 sp, ch 3, (2 dc, ch 2, 3 dc) in same sp, ★ (3 dc, ch 2,3 dc) in next ch 2 sp. Repeat from ★ around, join in top of beginning ch 3.
- **Rnd 37**: sl st to ch 2 sp, ch 3, 8 dc in same sp, ★ 9 dc in next ch 2 sp. Repeat from ★ around. Join. Fasten off.

First Ruffle

- **Rnd 1**: With neck edge of dress toward you, join white with sl st in first unused lp of Rnd 25, ch 3, (dc, ch 2, 2 dc) in same sp, sk 2 lps, ★(2 dc, ch 2, 2 dc) in next lp, sk 2 lps. Repeat from ★ around, join in top of beg ch 3 (47 shells).
- **Rnds 2–3**: Repeat Rnds 36-37 of Bottom Ruffle.

Second Ruffle

- Join white with sl st in first unused lp of Rnd 19. Repeat Rnds 1–3 of First Ruffle (34 shells).

Third Ruffle

- **Rnd 1**: Join white with sl st in first unused lp of Rnd 13, ch 3, (dc, ch 2, 2 dc) in same lp, sk lp, ★(2 dc, ch 2, 2 dc) in next lp, sk lp. Repeat from ★ around, join (15 shells).
- **Rnds 2-3**: Repeat Rnds 36-37 of Bottom Ruffle.

Sleeves

- **Rnd 1**: Join orange with sl st in 3rd ch at underarm, ch 1, sc in same sp and in next ch, sc in next 2 sc, 2 sc in each of next 4 sc, sc in next 2 sc, sc in last 2 ch at underarm, join, ch 1 (16 sc).
- **Rnds 2–4**: sc in each sc around, join, ch 1. (16 sc)
- **Rnd 5**: ★ sc in next 2 sc, dec next 2 sc. Repeat from ★ around, join, ch 1. (12 sc)
- **Rnd 6** - Repeat Rnd 5. (8 sc) Fasten off orange.
- **Rnd 7** - Join white with st in same sp as joining, ch 3, 6 dc in same sp, sk 1 sc, ★ 7 dc in next sc, sk 1 sc.

Repeat from ★ around, join with sl st in top of ch 3. Fasten off.

Edging of neck

- Join white with sl st in first st at neckline, ch 1, sc in same sp and in each ch across, ch 1, sl st in same sp as last sc was made. Fasten off.

Finishing dress

- Sew 2 buttons to back opening. Loop buttons through opening in stitches to close back of dress.
- Thread 1 yd. white ribbon through 1 st at each side of waist at underarms. Tie into bow at back.

Hat

- **Rnd 1**: With orange, ch 2, 6 sc in 2nd ch from hook, do not join. Mark beg of rnd here or as directed.
- **Rnd 2**: 2 sc in each sc around. (12 sc)
- **Rnd 3**: ★ sc in next sc, 2 sc in next sc. Repeat from ★ around. (18 sc)
- **Rnd 4**: ★ sc in next 2 sc, 2 sc in next sc. Repeat from ★ around. (24 sc)
- **Rnd 5**: ★ sc in next 3 sc, 2 sc in next sc. Repeat from ★ around. (30 sc)
- **Rnd 6**: ★ sc in next 4 sc, 2 sc in next sc. Repeat from ★ around. (36 sc)
- **Rnd 7**: ★ sc in next 5 sc, 2 sc in next sc. Repeat from ★ around, join, ch 1. (42 sc)
- **Rnd 8**: working in bl opp, sc in each sc around, join, ch 1. (42 sc)
- **Rnds 9–12**: sc in each sc around, join, ch 1. Fasten off orange at end of row 12. (42 sc)
- **Rnd 13**: join white with sl st in same sp as joining, ch 3, (dc, ch 2, 2 dc) in same sp, sk 1 sc, ★ (2 dc, ch 2, 2 dc) in next sc, sk 1 sc. Repeat from ★ around, join in top of beg ch 3.
- **Rnd 14**: sl st into ch 2 sp, ch 3, 6 dc in same sp, ★ 7 dc in next ch 2 sp. Repeat from ★ around, join. Fasten off.

Finishing Hat

- With 1 yd. white ribbon, beginning at center back, weave ribbon through sts of Rnd 7. Tie a bow.

Calling all girls! Placed on a pillow or set on a shelf, this little dolly will go straight to the heart of *your* little dolly.

Chapter 3

General Crafts

Everything is a Craft Project

The Fifties were a veritable craft-o-rama. The gung-ho energy and technological innovations of the times inspired people to put a spin on every craft they could. Bright colors replaced neutrals and free-form shapes squeezed out the traditional patterns. Newly available compounds such as plastics enabled home crafters to create things they never could before. And boy, oh boy, did they ever create!

The crafting craze gained nothing but steam over the following decades. Kits for making projects walked off store shelves. Yet as popular as these items were, crafters still looked for ways to reuse household items, resulting in wonderful—and weird—inventions.

Add a little life to any room

Original frames increase the value of paint-by-number paintings. To clean your painting, use mild soap and water and a soft cloth. Dry thoroughly.

Paint-by-number

A postwar phenomenon, paint-by-number kits promised that anyone could paint like the masters, a statement that was hotly debated.

"All you have to do to start is buy a kit. No lessons by correspondence. No classes in art. The outlay in money is very little." This quote from an early 1950s article in the *Chicago Sun Times* heralded the postwar craze of paint-by-numbers. A few containers of oil paints, a paintbrush and a canvas full of numbers was all that the aspiring artist needed.

The kits were the brainchild of Dan Robbins, a package designer for Palmer Paint Company. Robbins's inspirations for the kits were his childhood pastimes of coloring and painting, as well as a story of Michelangelo. It is said the painter assigned prenumbered sections of his works for his students to paint. Palmer Paint Company unveiled its paint-by-number kit concept, Craft Master, in 1951 at the American International Toy Show in New York, with promises that anyone "could be a Rembrandt."

"But, is it art?" This question caused heated debate in established art circles of the time. Whatever people felt about the legitimacy of this new art form, the general public went wild for it. Within the first three years, sales of the kits were in the tens of millions of dollars.

Over the next two decades, more companies offered paint-by-number sets. The kits featured images ranging from kittens, flowers, and comic book characters to landscapes and The Last Supper. The finished paintings were staples of American home decorating.

Though no longer the must-have of every crafter, paint-by-number sets are still widely available, now with acrylic paints. Today, the hobby's chief draw lies in the buying and selling of vintage paint-by-number kits, finished pictures, and accessories. The price and value of completed paintings and vintage kits may be affected by such factors as the number of kits for a particular design the manufacturer produced, whether the painting has its original frame, and if the artist's signature is present. Because paint-by-number items are relatively new collectibles, it's still possible for someone on a budget to build a collection.

It's as easy as 1•2•3

"It's so simple that it's almost kindergartenish!"

Glamour comes easy with...

Our groovy example of string art (right) has the funky black and way-out orange that would have made it perfect for a 1970's bedroom setting (above).

String art . . . that fabulous 1970s fad

Order. Symmetry. String art calls to those who crave these things—and who have the patience and time to engage in this exacting craft form. In the Seventies, everyone from summer campers and craft fairgoers to geometry students stretched bits of string to create abstract shapes and representational images such as butterflies, buildings, owls, ships, and sunbursts.

Though string art kits were widely available, one needed only a few common household items such as a piece of board, a bit of velvet, a hammer and nails, and of course, string. Feel the irresistible pull of this undeniably classic craft? Here are a few simple guidelines to get you started.

String Art

For a long-lasting picture, wrap strings tightly around nails. Patience pays off with beautiful results.

Materials

- **Colored pencils**
- **Fabric**
- **Hammer**
- **Masking tape**
- **Nails**
- **Paint**
- **Paper**
- **Protractor**
- **Sandpaper**
- **Spray adhesive**
- **String**
- **Varnish**
- **White craft glue**
- **Wood**

Instructions

1. Decide on design.

2. Draw design on paper and mark paper at spots where nails will go. Use colored pencils to mark areas where different colored strings will be used.

3. Prepare wood board. When painting board, choose a contrasting color to set off string. Sand wood to smooth, paint, let dry, then varnish. Let dry completely before adding nails. If covering with fabric (velvet is the most popular choice), cut fabric, leaving a 2" border all the way around. Apply spray adhesive and smooth fabric onto board. Bring fabric around sides and secure to back of board.

4. Tape pattern to front of prepared board.

5. Hammer a nail into each point on pattern. To keep all nails at the same height, use a precut piece of cardboard as a gauge.

6. When all nails have been added, pull off pattern.

7. Tie the end of the string to the first nail, using an overhand knot. String along as desired, using more loops for depth. When finished, tie off the string. Wrap the string around nail twice, make a loop in the string and twist the loop around your finger twice. Slip loop over top of nail, a pull string to tighten loop. Cut end of string close to nail and tuck end out of sight. Glue end to keep in place.

Dress up a plain wooden box with vintage jewels. For the look you see here, make sure to pack gems tightly together. Fill empty spaces with glitter or tiny painted rocks.

Jeweled Box

For her, a treasure box is as lovely as the trinkets she stores inside. Forgotten earrings?
Forgotten no more. Bracelets, necklaces, rings, and pins? Nested snug and secure until she's ready for them.
And when she's not—it sparkles beautifully. Just like her.

Materials

- Felt
- Glitter
- Industrial-strength craft glue
- Small oval craft mirror
- Vintage earrings, necklaces, pins, and pendants
- Wooden box

Instructions

1. Coat top of box with glue and center mirror on top of box. Allow glue to dry.
2. Glue jewelry to box one piece at a time until desired look is achieved.
3. Allow to dry 24 hours before handling box.
4. Cut felt to fit bottom of box. Attach felt with glue and allow to dry.

Note: The felt will protect surfaces from scratches.

Vintage jewelry can be purchased for pennies

AT THRIFT STORES AND FLEA MARKETS

THE FAMILY JEWELS

glittering symbol of holiday cheer

If you are lucky, you may stumble across a jeweled Christmas tree picture in an antique or thrift store, or have one created especially for you by an artist or loved one. This jeweled wonder awakens the holiday spirit in those who gaze upon it. If you have a box full of unused earrings, bracelets, and necklaces, a jeweled Christmas tree is a wonderful project to make.

Materials

- Chalk
- Foam-core board
- Jewelry, beads, and other sparkly items
- Picture frame
- Quick-drying jewelry glue
- Spray adhesive
- Velvet or other dark, heavy-weight fabric

Instructions

1. Apply spray adhesive to foam-core board.
2. Cover surface of board with fabric, smoothing out air bubbles with your hands.
3. Draw outline of tree on fabric with chalk.
4. Using a jewelry glue, adhere a string of beads to the chalk outline.
5. Fill in the outline as desired with jewelry, beads, and other jewel-like items.
6. Use strands of faux pearls as garlands and earrings as ornaments at end of branches.
7. Let picture dry 24 hours before framing.

"Even I was amazed!" says Wendi Wolfard.

The framed Christmas tree, made by designer Wendi Wolfard, was created with pieces Wendi collected from her two sisters, her parents, grandparents, cousins, aunts, and friends. She arranged them into this memory-filled and most wonderful symbol of the holidays.

This year give the Hep Cat gift...

Have a very cool Christmas with our mod electric candles. Top-of-the-line craft mesh and wired paper leaves will gleam in that dreamy holiday glow. These truly are tomorrow's Christmas candles. . . today.

DADDY-O CHRISTMAS CANDLES

Made with electric candle parts, these Christmas candles are very kitsch. Wired paper leaves are wound around the base.

MATERIALS

- 3 brass electric candle bases
- 3 electric candle kits, in varying sizes
- 3 lamp post cords with in-line switches
- Colored bulbs
- Wire craft mesh, gold
- Wired paper leaves, gold

INSTRUCTIONS

1. Put together candlesticks, bases, and cords as directed by manufacturer.
2. Wrap wire mesh around each candlestick. Cut to fit with ½" extra to wrap ends together—like you would a twist-tie.
3. Wrap leaves around base of each candlestick.
4. Insert the bulbs.

This year, make wrapping a Snap!

The Christmas he'll never forget . . . When ordinary wrapping paper simply won't do . . . nestle his gift in a wine crate, tie it up with a bright ribbon, and watch his eyes dance with glee. (You'll thank us for it later.)

The CHRISTMAS WINE BOX

The only wrapping he may appreciate more than the gift.

67

To be a real Hep Cat, your next party needs...

"The ladies go wild for my pin beaded fruit," confesses man-about-town Rex Thornton. "All I do is purchase soft plastic apples, lemons, pears, and grapes and give them a little magic."

Pin Beaded Fruit

Materials
- Red and gold sequins
- 2mm Seed beads
- Straight pins
- Thimble
- Variety of soft plastic fruit

Instructions

1. Beginning at top center of fruit, add one 2mm seed bead and one sequin onto pin and insert pin into fruit.

2. Continue around until you have made a tight circle of pins.

3. Continue making rows, slightly overlapping sequins as you go until entire fruit is covered. Make sure no plastic shows between sequins.

Imagine. Beauty that lasts forever. Style so easy, so durable. It's as close as your table when you fill a bowl with beaded fruit.

68

HORSING AROUND WITH WOOD

Throughout the 1960s, the popularity of crafting grew and ordinary people tackled projects that were previously reserved for professionals. This was especially true of woodworking; whether it was a cabinet, chair, or box, no project was too difficult. Types of woodworking included carving, scrollwork, and cabinetry. From suburban moms to urban hippies, it seems everyone at least tried to craft something from wood.

Woodworking is time consuming, but there is a sense of pride and accomplishment that comes when a project, large or small, is completed.

Women have continued the woodworking trend, and it is not unusual to spot the fair gender roaming the aisles of home improvement stores and lumber yards. While creating larger items can take hefty economic and time investments, small items like the sewing box seen here can be made inexpensively in just a few hours. Imagine how satisfied you will feel after finishing an item built for a lifetime of pleasure.

This sewing box was made using a few different techniques, including scrollwork, basic cabinetry, and a bit of carving. Made in the 1960s, this fine horse has withstood the test of time.

The posts hold spools of thread, while bobbins and needles can be stored out of sight. Lots of sanding to smooth edges of the wood ensures that the drawer fits just right, yet opens easily and stays closed.

no room is complete without a
resin grape cluster

Back in the 1960s and 1970s, your coffee table just wasn't presentable without a gleaming bunch of resin grapes resting on it! Resin casting was a new and exciting craft, and women whiled away hours creating home accessories such as ashtrays, paperweights, and (most memorably) grapes . . . or pineapples.

Resin casting continues to be a pleasurable and satisfying craft. The basic materials you need are easy to find and relatively inexpensive. Technology has improved casting and mold products, making it easier than ever to achieve the lustrous look of these gorgeous grapes.

In its liquid form, casting resin has a consistency of corn syrup and a slight color ranging from straw to light aqua. The period of time between the addition of the catalyst and the gel stage is called the working time. This stage lasts approximately 15–20 minutes. Do not catalyze more resin than you can pour during the working time since catalyzed resin cannot be poured once it has gelled.

The Commandments of Resin Casting

A Few Simple Rules for Successful Casts

- Follow manufacturer's directions and cautions on product labels.
- Always work in a well-ventilated room with temperatures from 65°F to 75°F.
- Always wear disposable gloves when working with resin. In addition, use tweezers when doing a project that requires dipping three-dimensional decorative elements into catalyzed resin.
- Always use a clean mixing container and stir stick for each batch of resin you mix.
- Use scratch-free, clean, and dry molds.

- Use acetone or rubbing alcohol to clean up liquid casting resin.
- Never pour catalyzed resin back into the resin can.
- Never work with casting resin around food or on food-handling surfaces.
- Never pour excess resin in sink; it will harden and clog the drain.
- Never disturb a casting until it has thoroughly cured.
- Keep all resin craft products—catalyst, dyes, pigments—out of the reach of children. Store resin in a dark place at room temperature (between 65°F and 75°F).

Complements any Room!

Resin grapes have been highly collectible for the past few years. From simple clusters to elaborate lamps and candelabra, they are available in many forms. Use a cluster as a bold statement on a table, fill bowls with them and place throughout the house, or deck out a patio with grapes of all sizes.

Dye grapes to match your décor, or choose colors of grapes to collect.

Grape Mistakes

Layers in a casting must not be allowed to fully cure until the final layer has been poured. A fully cured layer will shrink away from the sides of the mold, thus allowing additional pours to run down the sides of the previous layers. If this occurs, it would take a lengthy sanding and polishing job to correct. Or you could just start over!

Important Note: Read all instructions before starting your project.
This includes manufacturer's cautions as well as project directions.

Materials & Instructions

- Casting resin
- Catalyst
- Clear acrylic resin spray sealer
- Covered wire, cut into 10" lengths
- Disposable gloves
- Disposable graduated paper mixing cups
- Driftwood for stem
- Mold

- Newspapers (optional)
- Plastic sheeting
- Plastic wrap (optional)
- Resin dye
- Tape (optional)
- Varnish
- Waxed paper (optional)
- Wooden craft sticks

1. Gather all materials before starting the project.

2. Cover a level working surface with plastic sheeting. Several layers of waxed paper secured over newspapers or sheets of plastic wrap taped to the work surface will also work.

3. Make sure mold is clean and dry. Allow plastic molds to air-dry to avoid scratches; nonplastic molds may be dried with a lint-free cloth or paper towel.

4. Put on disposable gloves.

5. Measure resin. To determine the amount of resin required for mold, fill the mold with water, then pour water into a measuring cup. This is the total amount of resin that will be needed. *Note: Never use a plastic measuring cup to measure resin; plastic will melt on contact with resin.*

6. Pour the appropriate amount of casting resin into disposable mixing cup.

7. Add dye one drop at a time until the desired shade is achieved. Generally, 2–3 drops of dye per ounce of resin will provide the intensity desired. Too much dye will inhibit the cure of the resin. The color will look darker in the cup than in the casting, due to the depth of the container. Using a craft stick, stir well to blend.

8. Add catalyst. Following resin manufacturer's label directions, add the appropriate amount of catalyst to the casting resin. *Note: It is very important to be exacting in this step to assure proper curing.*

9. Mix thoroughly. Using a craft stick, mix resin and catalyst thoroughly for at least one minute. Scrape the sides and bottom of cup with stir stick to ensure proper mixing of resin and catalyst.

10. Pour resin mixture into mold, filling mold about ¾" full. Make sure mold is level before pouring. Do not pick up or move the mold once you have poured the first layer.

11. Allow first pour to gel. Resin will gel to consistency of set gelatin in approximately 15–25 minutes. Through hole at top of mold, test the surface with a craft stick. There must be sufficient firmness to support the weight of the wire. If surface has not reached a firm gel, wait a few more minutes and test again.

12. Roll end of covered wire as shown in Diagram A. This will prevent wire from being pulled out of completed grape.

Diagram A

13. When first pour has gelled, fill remainder of mold with resin. Immediately, but slowly insert wire, rolled end down. You will feel wire stop at top of first pour. Use tape to hold wire in place as shown in Diagram B. Remember to keep mold still as you work.

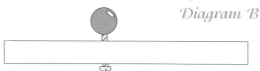

Diagram B

14. Allow resin cast to cure for the manufacturer's recommended length of time. During the curing process, the catalyzed resin goes through a series of stages: from a liquid to a soft gel in 15–20 minutes; from a soft gel to a firm gel in 20–30 minutes and finally to a hard (cured) stage in 1–24 hours. The length of this cycle varies greatly, depending on the size of mold poured. When cured, the edges of the cast shrink away from the sides of the mold. To minimize blemishes and fingerprints, do not handle casting until it is absolutely dry.

15. Remove casting from mold. Over a clean sheet of plastic, turn mold over. Flex mold as you would an ice cube tray. *Note: The cast should drop out of the mold.*

16. Repeat Steps 4–15 until you have completed enough grapes to make a cluster.

17. To remove minor blemishes, spray with several coats of clear acrylic sealer.

18. Sand and varnish driftwood. Let varnish dry completely.

19. Wrap wire stems around wood into desired cluster shape.

Grapes Even Go in the Kitchen!

Make Your Own GRAPE MOLDS

...for all your <u>TOUGH</u> grape needs

Of course, the easiest way to create resin grapes is by using a premade round silicone mold. If you have difficulty finding a suitable mold, be crafty and make one yourself. Make sure to have at least one mold for each size of grape you will create. There are many types; just be sure to use one that is suitable for use with casting resin. Choose a cup that is wide enough to have ½" of free space all around the ball and deep enough to allow pouring 1" of material above the ball.

Materials

- Electric drill and ¹⁄₁₆" bit
- Measuring cup
- Molding material
- Plastic drinking cup
- Plastic modeling clay
- Sandpaper
- Sharp craft knife
- Silicone release agent
- Varnish
- Wood board, 12" x 12"
- Wood screw, #10
- Wood wax
- Wooden ball(s)

Instructions

1. Sand wooden ball(s) to smooth surface. Varnish ball to seal surface and create blemish-free mold. Allow varnish to dry.
2. Drill a ¹⁄₁₆" hole in the center of ball.
3. Sand top surface of wood board; varnish and allow to dry.
4. Wax top surface of wood board.
5. From back of board, "drill" the wood screw through wood.
6. Set the small hole end of ball on exposed screw and twist two times to secure onto screw.
7. Cut out the bottom of the plastic drinking cup with craft knife and secure it to the waxed wood surface with plastic clay, using a strip (also known as a bead) of clay approximately ¾" thick.
8. Spray the ball with silicone release agent and allow to dry, approximately 30 minutes.
9. Mix enough molding material to fill the plastic cup around the ball. Measure exact amount needed by putting the ball into a same-sized cup and filling cup with water. Remove ball from water. Pour water into measuring cup. The amount of water in the measuring cup is the amount of mold material needed, plus 10 percent for slack.
10. Pour molding material around the ball to fill the cup at lease ¾" above the ball. Allow to cure for manufacturer's recommended time.
11. When mold is cured, remove the cup from wood base and push the silicone mold out. With craft knife, and using the screw hole as a guide, slice down to just above the halfway point on both sides. Remove ball. Using the knife again, enlarge the screw hole to at least ½" diameter.

PINEAPPLE LAMP

For reasons that may never be fully explained or understood, truly kitschy crafts are endearing. Liking them is akin to picking the homeliest puppy of the litter. You love it because it isn't pretty. Our pineapple lamp falls into that category. So wrong, it's right. So bad, it's cool. Everything needed for this project can be purchased at lamp supply or craft stores.

Materials

- 4 hex nut/lock washers to fit lamp post
- 16 resin grapes, 8 each of 2 different sizes.
- Candelabrum bulb
- Lamp base
- Lamp post cord with in-line switch
- Light socket with candelabrum base
- Plastic pineapple leaves
- Straight pipe, 7" long, threaded ⅛" on each end
- Washer to fit lamp post, 2"

Instructions

1. Attach one nut/lock washer to lamp post. Turn until it rests 1½" from end.

2. Insert screw end of lamp post into base. Attach second nut/lock washer to post underneath base. Tighten.

3. Attach one nut/lock washer to top of post, 1" from top. Attach 2" washer. *Note: This will act as a platform for leaves. On top of washer, attach nut/lock washer.*

4. Starting from bottom of lamp, thread cord through post. Attach candelabrum base as directed on package. Insert bulb. For now, let rest on top of post.

5. Wrap four of the smaller grapes around lamp post. *Note: This is the bottom layer.*

6. Make two layers of four grapes, using larger sized grapes. Leave a 1" space between grapes and post. *Note: Light will fit behind grapes.*

7. *Make one layer of small grapes on top.*

8. Gently pull up on socket/cord until you have approximately 2" of cord at top. Tuck cord and light between layers of grapes, making sure light is behind grapes.

9. Tuck plastic leaves along top of lamp.

Grapes are simply wrapped around lamp post. Light is tucked behind grapes and can be turned on and off with a pull-cord switch.

PLASTIC PINEAPPLE LEAVES ARE SIMPLY TUCKED ALONG THE TOP OF THE LAMP AFTER THE LAMP IS PUT TOGETHER.

Perfect for girls of all ages,

you can make matching mom-and-daughter purses by adding packets to the pattern.

JUICE PACKET
Purse

All You Need
- 9 empty juice packets
- Sewing machine
- Thread

Kicky and bright, the Juice Packet Purse is durable too. Just be careful to not store sharp or hot items inside. Make sure the bright pictures face the outside. Purse is easily cleaned using soap and water.

EASY TO FOLLOW INSTRUCTIONS

1. Cut a slit in the bottom of each pack-et. Wash inside and out with warm water and soap. Let dry.
2. Front: Set two packets side by side and sew a zigzag stitch down the middle to connect them. as shown in Diagram A.
3. Fold top over enough to cover the straw hole and sew a straight line from one end to the other.
4. Back: Repeat Steps 2 and 3. This will be the back side of the purse.
5. Bottom: Overlap two more packets so they are the same length as the front side. Sew across the tops of the packets as shown in Diagram B.
6. Side: Take one packet and lay it on the bottom of the purse. Make a zigzag stitch across the edge. as shown in Diagram C)
7. Repeat Step 3.

8. Repeat Steps 6 and 7 for the remaining side.
9. Handle: Take one packet and cut it across the middle horizontally.
10. Fold one side of packet to center. Fold opposite edge over this. Make sure pattern shows on outside of handle.
11. Sew a seam down each side horizon-tally. Repeat for both halves.
12. Sew the two bottoms together.
13. Take the bottom and the sides of the bag and sew the handle to the center of the right side. Repeat for left side. as shown in Diagram D.
14. Take the front piece of the purse and lay it on the bottom of the purse so that the edges are together. Sew the bottom first, then move to the sides, as shown in Diagram E.
15. Repeat for the back of purse.

Diagram A

Diagram B

Diagram C

Diagram D

Diagram E

77

CRAFTING & FINE ART
THE ART

TECHNIQUES

- Cut paper results in a more detailed collage and works well for designs requiring small paper pieces or defined edges, such as buildings or geometric shapes.

- Torn paper lends a softer quality to collage. This technique allows the blending and layering of colors. Jagged mountain tops, wind-whipped seascapes, wispy clouds—all can be produced with torn papers.

- Blending techniques brings endless possibilities, from garden scenes to kites flying against a beautiful blue sky.

- It is always a good idea to work with the materials prior to embarking on your project. Tear and cut small pieces of the papers you will use and play with gluing, layering, and placement.

Sophisticated and stunning, collage slipped onto the 1960s scene through artists such as Andy Warhol, Joseph Cornell, and Eric Carle. Intriguing crafters of all ages and abilities, collage unlocked the creativity of many who lacked painting and drawing skills. You, too, may find your genius in blending papers subtle and transparent or thick and bold.

BECOME CLOSE COMPANIONS

OF PAPER COLLAGE

Abstract tiger lilies bloom in our collage (opposite). Rip and layer transparent rice and tissue papers for a soft look; create more defined shapes with heavier papers.

MATERIALS

- Acrylic brush, 1"-wide
- Clear-drying glue
- Cloth or soft tissues
- Papers of various colors and types
- Pencil
- Plywood or white canvas board
- Ruler
- Scissors
- Spray sealer
- Wood primer (if using plywood)

INSTRUCTIONS FOR GLUING

Tear or cut the first piece of paper and place it on the plywood or canvas background. Use the pencil to lightly mark its position. Remove paper. Brush marked area with glue. Apply paper to wet glue and brush additional glue over the top of paper, removing air bubbles as you go. *Note: Small wrinkles will add a desirable texture to your design.* Repeat until design is complete. Wrap paper beyond edges and glue to sides and back to finish.

- Using wood for a background? Seal it with primer and let dry before you start your collage.
- Want special effects? Try brushing a little water onto the edges of your papers to get the colors to bleed.
- Need protection? When finished collage is dry, cover it with an additional coat of glue. Allow it to dry, then apply spray sealer.

Gifts from the Sea

VINTAGE SEASHELL CRAFTS

"Leave no shell unturned!" was the rallying cry of the American crafter in the middle of the twentieth century. Families returned from seaside vacations with boxes of precious shells, coral, and starfish and one thing on their minds: bringing the beauty and happy memories of their time by the ocean into their homes. For the busy Mr. and Mrs., gift shops provided the coveted ornaments with ready-made convenience.

If you have a yearning for shell crafting, here are a few tips:

- When using shells collected on the beach, be sure to clean shells thoroughly before using.

- If there is any dirt left on the shell's surface, simply scrape with a soft brush and wipe clean with a soft cloth. Then carefully soak your sea treasures in a solution of one part chlorine bleach to four parts water.

- Shells will need to be dried thoroughly before using in crafts. Either let them dry in the sun or, if you are in a hurry, speed drying time with a fan or blow dryer.

Some Crafty Ideas

All That Glitters
Cover miniature shoes with a layer of glue, sprinkle a mixture of sand and glitter onto the shoes. Let glue dry. Glue miniature shells and tiny gems to shoes. Let glue dry.

Wind chimes
Drill a hole in the edge of several shells or purchase predrilled shells from craft store. String shells on fishing line or thin twine and tie to a hanger. Wind chimes can be simple or very intricate. Be sure to space the strings of shells so that they don't tangle, then hang in a sunny spot.

Scented shell potpourri
Clean shells, brush scented oil on surface of shells and place shells in a basket.

Bring your holiday home with strings of seashells. Hang them with a clear plastic liner for a curtain that makes each shower seem like a splash in the ocean.

80

Pssst! Have you heard about seashell crafts?

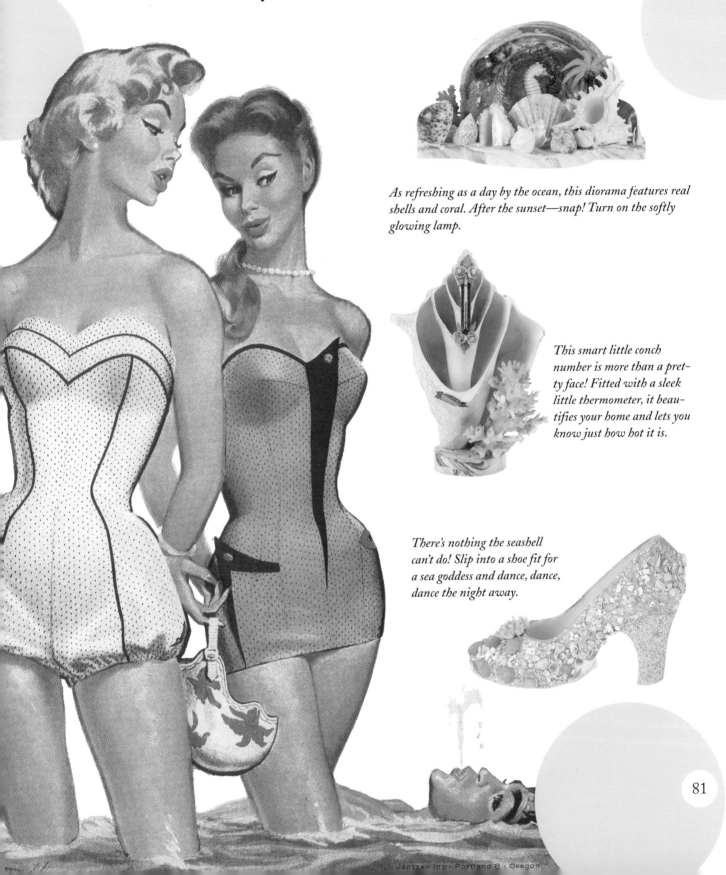

As refreshing as a day by the ocean, this diorama features real shells and coral. After the sunset—snap! Turn on the softly glowing lamp.

This smart little conch number is more than a pretty face! Fitted with a sleek little thermometer, it beautifies your home and lets you know just how hot it is.

There's nothing the seashell can't do! Slip into a shoe fit for a sea goddess and dance, dance, dance the night away.

81

Monkey

Boys and girls of all ages love their sock monkeys!

Though this classic creation wasn't truly popular until the Great Depression, children have been embracing their sock monkeys for more than a century. Their appeal stayed strong all through the postwar era as thrifty moms continued to transform leftover socks into lovable toys. By the Seventies, sock manufacturers were selling sock monkey kits for 50 cents.

People are as crazy about sock monkeys as ever. See them on exhibit in major museums and pop-art paintings, read about them in comic books and adventure stories. Or grab a sock, a little stuffing, and get started. It's as fun as a barrel of—you know.

instructions

Made With

- Buttons or felt for eyes
- Needle and thread
- Scraps for clothes
- Scissors
- Socks, 2

Sock A

1. Turn one sock inside out.
2. Body: Beginning 3" from heel of sock, sew two seams ½" from outer edge of sock up to and across top of sock. Top of seam should be slightly rounded as shown in Diagram A. Cut sock between the seams sewn. End cut at bottom of seams. *Note: This will leave an opening in the crotch.*
3. Turn sock right side out. Use opening to stuff the head, body, and legs. Sew seam closed.

Sock B

1. Arms: Cut upper part of sock into two pieces as shown in Diagram B. Sew the seam along each side, rounding the ends, and stuff the arms. Stitch arms to body.
2. Mouth: Cut heel from sock as shown in Diagram B. Using a whipstitch, stitch bottom of heel to lower part of face, stuff, and finish sewing in place. To give the monkey character, stitch a running stitch across middle of lips.
3. Tail: Cut a 1" strip tapered to end of toe as shown in Diagram B. Sew seam along side and stuff. Stitch tail to lower back of body.
4. Ears: Cut ear pieces from remaining sock. *Note: Ears can be of any size or shape desired—he is your creation after all!* If desired stuff ears. Stitch ears to body.
5. Eyes: Stitch on buttons, or felt, for eyes, or embroider with black or brown thread. *Note If monkey is to be played with by small children, use felt or embroider the eyes.*
6. Hat: A hat can be created from the heel of another sock. Fezzes are a popular choice for sock monkey hats.

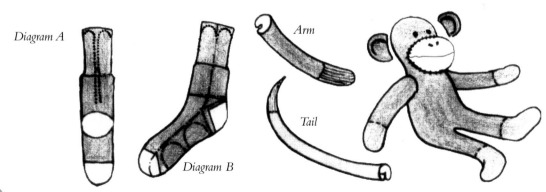

Diagram A *Arm* *Tail* *Diagram B*

Business

ADORABLE

UNBREAKABLE

The heart-stealing doll is easy to create and can be made from any socks you choose. The monkey is dressed in clothes made from fabric scraps. His hat, tie, and socks are also made from a sock.

EASY & FUN!

THERE'S AN EASIER AND MORE PERSONAL WAY TO RECORD THE DAY'S EVENTS

New **FABRIC-COVERED JOURNAL**

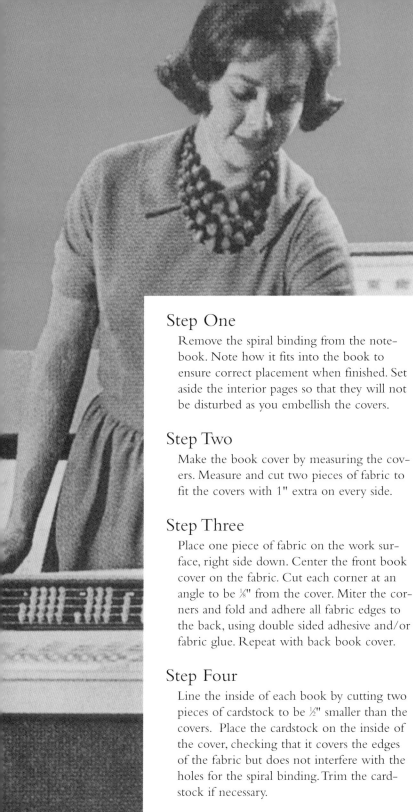

Materials

- Cardstock
- Craft knife
- Double sided adhesive
- Fabric glue
- Fabric to cover both sides of each cover
- Heavy book
- Pins or clips
- Rickrack
- Ruler
- Scissors
- Seed beads
- Spiral-bound notebook
- Wire cutter
- Wire for seed beads

Step One

Remove the spiral binding from the notebook. Note how it fits into the book to ensure correct placement when finished. Set aside the interior pages so that they will not be disturbed as you embellish the covers.

Step Two

Make the book cover by measuring the covers. Measure and cut two pieces of fabric to fit the covers with 1" extra on every side.

Step Three

Place one piece of fabric on the work surface, right side down. Center the front book cover on the fabric. Cut each corner at an angle to be ⅛" from the cover. Miter the corners and fold and adhere all fabric edges to the back, using double sided adhesive and/or fabric glue. Repeat with back book cover.

Step Four

Line the inside of each book by cutting two pieces of cardstock to be ½" smaller than the covers. Place the cardstock on the inside of the cover, checking that it covers the edges of the fabric but does not interfere with the holes for the spiral binding. Trim the cardstock if necessary.

Step Five

Cut the fabric covering to ½" larger than the inside piece and follow the instructions above to cover.

Step Six

Measure enough rickrack to make an edge for the cover, adding 1". Place the rickrack along three edges of the cover, leaving the side for the spiral binding free. Glue rickrack into place with fabric glue. Turn the ends of the trim over onto themselves for a neat finish. Use pins or clips to hold into place until dry.

Step Seven

Set the covered cardstock on the inside of each cover and glue down. Place a heavy book on each cover.

Step Eight

Add beads to the wire. Twist the beaded wire into a tight spiral to form the center of the flower. Shape the beaded wire into loops to form double petals. Twist the wire periodically to hold the flower together.

Step Nine

Adhere the flower to the cover of the book with glue. Cover with a heavy book and allow to dry.

Step Ten

Use the craft knife to open the holes for the spiral binding in the outside covers. Thread the spiral binding through the holes as originally placed.

Don't throw out those vinyl records! These swinging coasters are such a perfect take-away gift for party guests, you'll blast straight to the top of the charts!

Rocking Record Coasters

TO PROTECT LABEL, LAMINATE THE SURFACE OF EACH COASTER BEFORE FIRST USE

Sure, you could buy record coasters, but when you see how fun they are to make, you won't want to. And when you make your own, you choose the titles. That's right. To match the party theme, reflect the guest of honor's musical tastes, whatever. You decide. With your own Rocking Record Coasters, it's your party.

Materials

- Adhesive-backed cork or felt
- Adhesive-backed plastic film
- Drill with circular cutting attachment
- Oven
- Oven mitts
- Sandpaper
- Vinyl record

Instructions

1. Preheat oven to 210°F, place record on cookie sheet and put in oven to soften, approximately 5–10 minutes. Wearing oven mitts, remove from oven.

2. Using an electric drill with circular cutting attachment, and while record is still soft, carefully cut around the label in center of record, leaving approximately 1" of vinyl around label.

3. Sand edges to smooth.

4. Seal label with adhesive-backed plastic film to prevent lifting.

5. Draw outline of coaster on cork or felt. Cut to fit, peel off backing, and attach to back side of coaster to provide protection to tabletop surfaces.

RECORD SERVING BOWLS

E vening at home a little too quiet? Pop a platter on the hi-fi and shake some chips into your very own Record Serving Bowl. Once a way for clever hostesses to recycle records in the Fifties and Sixties, hip crafters carry on the fad with thrift store finds. (First checking out the value to avoid melting a fortune!) Of course, hot foods, hot liquids, and dishwashers are simply a no-go. But paired with a set of Rocking Record Coasters? They set the party spinning just fine.

For a personal statement, create your own labels, place over original label, then laminate.

Materials
- Adhesive-backed plastic film
- Oven
- Oven mitts
- Oven-safe bowls, 2
- Timer
- Vinyl record

Instructions
1. Preheat oven to 225°F.
2. Turn over bowl so it is bottom up. Place bowl on cookie sheet. Lay record on top of bowl, making sure record is centered.
3. Place bowl with record in oven. Stay close and watch as record heats up and begins to mold to the shape of the bowl (this will take only a minute). You may want to help shape the bowl with your hands, just remember to use oven mitts to prevent burns.
4. Remove bowl and record from oven. With covered hands, immediately remove record and place inside second bowl. This will help to keep the shape as bowl cools.
5. When bowl is cool, seal label with adhesive-backed plastic film to prevent lifting.

Record serving bowls get the party moving
Psst. Pack one up with tasty treats for a gift basket that's out of sight!

It's Far Out Baby

What craft could more effectively represent the 1970s—hippies, flower children, peace, and love—than tie-dye? It is truly synonymous with this free-spirited decade. Items from T-shirts, ties, and blue jeans to pillowcases and blankets were stitched, folded, tied, and colored into new creations.

88

Tie-dye for Home & Body

You thought you were original? Well you are. And so is every piece you tie-dye. Though this art form—also called "resistance dyeing"—has been around almost as long as human beings, the way you tie the fabric and place the dye is virtually impossible to duplicate. And that is a good thing.

Materials

- Bucket for dye bath
- Cotton thread for sewing resist patterns into fabric
- Cotton twine or rubber bands to bind fabric
- Disposable gloves
- Fabric (for best results, choose white or off-white)
- Fabric dye suitable for fabric chosen, 3 different colors (follow manufacturer's recommendations)
- Plastic bottles for applying dye to limited parts of fabric
- Plastic sheeting to cover work surfaces
- Sink with running water

Instructions for T-shirt

1. Starting in center of shirt, approximately 4" below neckline, pinch fabric and gather in a point.
2. Wrap twine tightly around neck of the gathered fabric, crossing the loose end to prevent slipping.
3. Wrap twine around a few times, knot, and cut ends of twine.
4. Repeat Steps 1–3, leaving 1"–2" between ties, until you reach the bottom.
5. Mix dye as directed. *Note: T-shirt was made with deep blue, lime, and fuchsia dyes.*
6. Apply dye to T-shirt. Squirt first dye color to top point of fabric. Add a bit of second dye color to same point of fabric. Squeeze fabric to mix dyes together. At the next section of fabric, use only first dye color. Dye the next few sections second dye color, then a few sections with third dye color. Now back to first dye color for one section. Finish by alternating colors. Mix colors to create varying effects.
7. Wrap T-shirt in plastic wrap and allow to set for recommended time.
8. Rinse fabric.Continue rinsing as you carefully cut knots. Be careful to not cut fabric as you remove twine.
9. Finish fabric as directed on dye package. Dry T-shirt.

Tie-dye T-Shirt

Unique, free-form designs made tie-dye T-shirts the ultimate expression of the Seventies spirit. Grab a white shirt and a little household dye and declare your own freedom with a spectacular celebration of color.

Tie-dye Pillowcase

Rest your head on soothing waves of blue. Two shades of blue make a white pillowcase look like something out of your most pleasant dreams.

Instructions for Pillowcases

Note: Two tying methods and dye baths were used on these pillowscases.
1. Bunch fabric together in a ball and randomly tie twine around fabric.
2. Dye pillowcases light blue according to manufacturer's directions.
3. Rinse fabric and untie.
4. Rinse fabric until water runs almost clear. Squeeze water out of fabric.
5. Fold fabric lengthwise, then fold into accordion pleats.
6. Tie fabric at 2" intervals down length of fabric.
7. Dye cases dark blue according to manufacturer's directions.
8. Rinse dye from pillowcases.
9. Continue rinsing as you carefully cut knots. Be careful to not cut fabric as you remove twine.
10. Finish as directed on dye package. Dry the pillowcases.

All Tied Up

Basic Fabric Tying Techniques

Outline

1. Pick up fabric where center of design is to be.

2. Gather the fabric where the outline will be.

3. Wind string around the neck of the gathered fabric, making sure to cross over loose end of string. *Note: This prevents slipping.*

4. Wrap string tightly around neck a few more times. Knot and cut ends.

Stripes

1. Fold a layer of fabric into accordion pleats, making sure to pleat evenly.

2. Gather pleated fabric where first strip is to appear.

3. Gather the fabric where the outline will be.

4. Wind string around the neck of the gathered fabric, making sure to cross over loose end of string. *Note: This prevents slipping.*

5. Wrap string tightly around neck a few more times. Knot and cut ends.

6. Repeat for desired effects.

7. For a more uniform stripe, wrap string closely; for a lacy effect, leave a bit of space between coils of string; for a strip within a stripe, wrap tightly, leave a bit of space, then wrap tightly again.

Starburst

1. Pick up fabric where center of design is to be.

2. Make a knot in fabric—the tighter the knot the greater the contrast of colors.

3. The distance from the top of point to the knot will determine the size of the sunburst.

Corner Design

1. Make a knot in each corner of fabric—the tighter the knot the greater the contrast of colors.

Stitching

1. Draw design on fabric with a soft pencil.

2. Make a line of running stitches along the design, using a double strand of white cotton thread. The tighter the stitch, the more defined the design will be.

3. Remove stitches after dye process.

Wine Bottle
Candleholder

You have a box of pizza and a bottle of wine. Your pad doesn't have furniture, so your friends sit on the floor. The conversation is so intense, you don't notice it's dark until someone lights a candle. And another one.

Next day, the people have gone and you think about the night. Maybe you didn't solve the world's problems. Maybe you did. That wine bottle, with its layers of wax, is your witness. If only it could talk.

Materials
- Interesting wine bottle
- Matches
- Nondripless tapers

Instructions
1. Trim bottom of candle to fit wine bottle.
2. Place candle in top of empty wine bottle.
3. Light the candle.

A bottle of Chianti—drained, of course—is the classic Seventies candleholder. Though any funky bottle can give you this look, check antique shops and thrift stores if vintage is what you want.

93

Put a little bite in your bathroom with . . .

CROCHETED TOILET PAPER COVER

A crocheted poodle keeps toilet paper out of sight—and takes you back in time to your Grandma's house. Believe it or not, art museums and needlework societies have held exhibits of the delightfully discrete faux pets, but you needn't hunt high and low to find one. Follow our simple pattern and make your own.

THE PERFECT ADDITION

MATERIALS

Buttons, or plastic eyes

Crochet hook, size G or H

Elastic, ½" wide, 2/3 yd.

Pom Poms, 8 (for ears, feet, top of head, and tail)

Yarn, 4 oz. for poodle, any color you choose

Yarn, 2 yd. for mouth and nose

INSTRUCTIONS

Gauge: 5dc and 5 sps = 2 inches

2 rounds = 1 inch

BODY

Beginning at center top, ch4. Join with sl st to form ring.

1st rnd: ch 4, (dc in ring, ch 10) 11 times. Join to 3rd ch of ch4.

2nd rnd: ch 4, picking up back loops only through-out, dc in joining, ch 1 dc in next dc, ch 1 ★ in next dc make (dc, ch 10 twice-1 sp increased, dc in next dc, ch1. Repeat from ★ around. Join as before.

Next 3 rnds: work as for 2nd. rnd, increasing 6 spaces evenly around (36 aps on 5th round).

Next 8 rounds: work as for 2nd round, omitting the increase. Break off and fasten at end of last rnd.

HEAD

Starting at center top, ch 2.

1st rnd: make 6 sc in 2nd ch from hook.

2nd rnd: 2 sc in each sc around

3rd rnd: ★sc in next sc, 2 sc in next sc (1 sc increased). Repeat from ★ around.

4th and 5th rnds: sc in each sc increasing 6 scs evenly spaced (30 sc on 5th rnd.). Work without increasing for 6 rnds.

Next 2 rnds: sc in each sc. Decreasing 6 sc evenly spaced, to dec 1 sc (insert hook in next sc, yarn over and draw loop through twice, yarn over and draw through all loops on hook).

Work 1 rnd without decreasing.

Next rnd: repeat 4th rnd. Work 1 rnd without increasing. Break off and fasten.

NOSE

Starting at tip with black. Ch 2

1st rnd: make 6 sc in 2nd ch from hook. Break off. Attach main color and work 2nd rnd as for 2nd rnd of head.

Next 4 rnds: sc in each sc around.

Break off and fasten at end of last rnd.

FINISHING B

Stuff head and nose with batting. Sew nose to head. Sew on buttons for eyes. *Note: You also may embroider eyes.* Sew one pom pom to top of head and one on each side for ears.

Sew bottom edge of head to top of body.

Sew pom pom legs and tail in place.

Fold elastic in half and thread through stitches at lower edge of body. Pull tightly to fit over the roll of tissue. Tie ends together.

My bathroom is...

Just Peachy

because of Peach Pit Grape Cluster

Don't toss that peach pit!
Collect a bunch and you've
got the perfect material for
carving, painting, and pro-
ducing fabulous items from
bracelets to decorations.
This versatile gift of nature
has a size and shape that
makes it a natural for creating this stunning peach pit
grape cluster.

Materials

- 60 clean dry peach pits
- 6 plastic grape leaves
- Craft glue
- Craft paint
- Craft wire
- Scissors
- Shallow bowl
- Surface sealer spray
- Wire cutters
- Wooden dowel, 8"–12"

Instructions

Clean peach pits and let dry.

- In a shallow bowl, pour a small amount of the desired color of paint you want for the "grapes."
- Drop the pits, a few at a time, into the paint. Roll them around until pit is covered with paint. Remove from bowl and let dry. Continue until all pits are painted.
- Seal painted pits with surface spray sealer. Let dry.
- Guide a piece of wire through the holes of a pit until pit is in center of wire. Continue until all pits are wired.
- Using the wooden dowel as the base, wrap wired pits around until the grape cluster is pleasing to the eye.
- Attach plastic leaves to cluster with craft glue.

Chapter 4

BEADING

From Natural to Glamorous

Ancients relied on them for magical powers and explorers traded them for goods. Victorians stitched them to clothes and hippies strung them from rafters. Starting with the first shell strung on seaweed to the finest creations of Venetian glassmakers, beads have long expressed the human love of adornment.

The art of beading evolves to reflect the changing times. The Fifties saw women beading domestic items such as baskets and cocktail jewelry from refined materials such as glass and plastic. In the Sixties and Seventies, a back-to-nature trend led people to prefer natural substances such as stone, clay, bone, and wood. Today, crafters can select their beads based on which era they wish to emulate.

It's easier than riding

Here are a few things you will need to purchase before starting your bead projects.

- Assorted beads
- Bead reamer
- Bead thread
- Bead wire
- Containers for beads
- Jewelry findings: clasps, crimps, earring backs, loops, etc.
- Needle threader
- Needle-nosed pliers
- Needles
- Pins
- Safety pins
- Scissors
- Thimble
- Wax

a bike.

Bead Basics

The successful beader has the patience and the dexterity to handle tiny objects for long stretches of time. To make your beading experience one worth repeating, follow these tips:

- Cover your work surface with a towel to catch stray beads.
- Sit in a comfortable chair—you're going to be there a while.
- Turn on a nice, bright light to prevent eyestrain.
- Consider using a needle threader—beading needles are thinner than sewing needles.
- Have a bead reamer on hand to smooth or widen the hole of a stubborn bead.
- Coat your string with beeswax for easier stringing.
- Experiment with different types of string, thread, and wire to discover the varied effects you can achieve.
- Take the time to plan your design and ensure you have all the materials you need before you begin— you'll find beading more enjoyable.
- Stop and stretch from time to time to avoid aches and pains.
- Select findings and other materials to complement the beads in your design for professional-looking results.
- Keep beads in easy-access containers, separated by color and size for faster beading.

The Finest of Family Gifts

A must-have for a lady's vanity, bureau, or nightstand, a Safety Pin Basket is a feminine treat (and now a hot collectible). Colorful beads transform the most humble Cinderella of household objects—the ordinary safety pin—into a jeweled princess of elegance and fashion. Can't find one of these beauties in a store? Make your own.

Symmetry is key when creating a safety pin basket. Prepare all pins prior to beginning project and count as you go.

Safety Pin Basket

Materials

20-gauge wire
27 8mm round faceted peach beads
68 6mm oval gold beads
98 #1 (1"–long) safety pins
162 8mm round faceted green beads
196 2mm gold beads
Needle-nosed pliers
Wire cutters

Instructions

Prepare beaded pins

1. Open all of the pins.
2. On each pin, thread one 2mm gold bead, one green bead, then one 2mm gold bead. Close the pin.

Make basket

Note: Unless otherwise indicated, place beaded side of each pin facing outside of basket.

Row 1: Using 18 pins, 9 green beads and 9 peach beads, string wire through tails of pins alternating with one green or one peach bead between each pin. Twist ends of wire together with beaded sides of pins facing out; cut wires.

Row 2: Using 9 pins and 9 green beads, string wire through head of Row 1 pin, tail of Row 2 pin, head of Row 1 pin, one green bead. Repeat this pattern around. Twist wires together and cut.

Row 3: Using 9 pins and 9 green beads, string wire through tail of Row 3 pin, tail of Row 3 pin, head of Row 2 pin, green bead. Repeat this pattern around. Twist wires together and cut.

Row 4: Using 18 pins and 18 green beads and placing beaded side of each pin facing in toward center of basket, string wire through tail of Row 4 pin, head of Row three pin, tail of Row 4 pin, bead, tail of Row 4 pin, head of Row 3 pin, tail of Row 4 pin, bead. Repeat this pattern around using two or more wires as needed for ease of stringing. Twist wires together and cut.

Row 5: Using 36 pins, 36 green beads and 18 peach beads and placing beaded side of each pin facing in toward center of basket, string wire through head of Row 4 pin, one peach bead, head of Row 4 pin, 2 green beads. Use as many short lengths of wire as needed for ease of stringing and shaping ruffle. Repeat pattern around. Twist wires together and cut.

Finish basket: Further shape ruffle with fingers as needed. Tighten wires as sections are shaped. Tighten all twisted wires and trim to ½". Bend wires to blend with basket.

Make handle

1. Attach and twist two wires between pairs of pins separated by two green beads on Row 4.
2. String one 6mm oval bead then one pin onto each wire.
3. String two oval beads and one pin onto each wire. Repeat 15 times.
4. String one bead onto each wire, attach and twist wires on opposite side of basket. Shape handle into arch. Shape basket into shape shown in photo.

The handle is added to basket at end of project. Make sure to tightly wrap wires to basket to prevent handles from coming loose.

Mother's Day — May 12TH

Give her the perfect gift this year from the whole family

SAFETY PIN NECKLACE

Safety pin art wasn't just prim and proper. It could also reflect the edgier attitudes of the changing times. In a design that mimics the primitive look of teeth strung on leather, this necklace is just raw enough to say "street smart" while gold cord, aqua beads, and a clever knotting technique also whisper "sophisticated."

Exposed safety pins give a piece a raw, slightly unfinished look that may be just what the modern girl needs.

Try this on for sighs?
BEADED TIE

A necktie for *her*? Why not—when it's as pretty as this beaded confection.
She'll be just as feminine as ever—and drawing curious eyes her way. Not for
the timid, not for the tame. Menswear, taken to places it's never been before.

Beaded Earrings & Pin

Man's best friend knows . . . a girl's best friend isn't a diamond. It's beads. Lots and lots of beads. Put them on a pin. Put them on earrings. Just put them on.

You'll be able to . . .
Pass the Love, Baby

with this timeless necklace

The year was 1967 and it was "The Summer of Love." To protest the Vietnam War, young people gathered with an idea to promote peace by seeing the sunny side of life. With the slogan "Make Love, Not War, " the Flower Child movement was born. Supporters donned colorful clothes and tucked flowers in their hair, sang protest songs, and strung necklaces of beads they traded and gave away freely as symbols of compassion and unity. These necklaces came to be called Love Beads, and were worn by women and men alike.

Materials

- Beading needle
- Heavy-weight nylon beading thread
- Quick-drying, industrial-strength glue
- Round glass beads, various colors, 12mm
- Seed beads, various colors, 2mm
- Seed beads, various colors, 6mm

Instructions

1. Measure thread for double the desired length of necklace. Thread the needle, then bring ends of thread together and knot, leaving a 3" tail at end of string.

2. String one 6mm bead onto thread and slide to knot.

3. String one 12mm bead onto thread, one 6mm bead, and at least 30 2mm beads.

4. Continue until end of necklace, leaving 3" tail at opposite end of necklace. Do not knot after last bead.

5. When last bead is in place, pull thread through the first bead. Place a knot around the thread between the first and second bead. Set end beads with glue to prevent unraveling.

The real difference in chic is
Her Beaded Necklace

For the lady whose tastes are more uptown than downtown, a pretty rope of pearlescent beads is just what she needs. Whether complementing a formal ensemble or adding a feminine touch to a casual outfit, beaded necklaces are all the rage.

Chapter 5

‖ Macramé ‖
the Creative Knot
An ancient art makes a comeback.

Macramé is the ancient art of knotting twine or string. Archeologists believe it originated in the Middle East and traveled through Europe. Sailors carried it across oceans and traded their macraméd creations for supplies at ports around the world. The practical value of this craft lies in the strength it lends natural fibers such as jute. Twining and knotting strands together reinforces them to create more reliable items such as hammocks. Most crafts, however, are drawn to macramé for its aesthetic value. Through the art of knotting, one can turn ordinary string, yarn, rope, or leather cord into a magnificent object of beauty.

110   I'm not finished untill I put on my *Macramé*

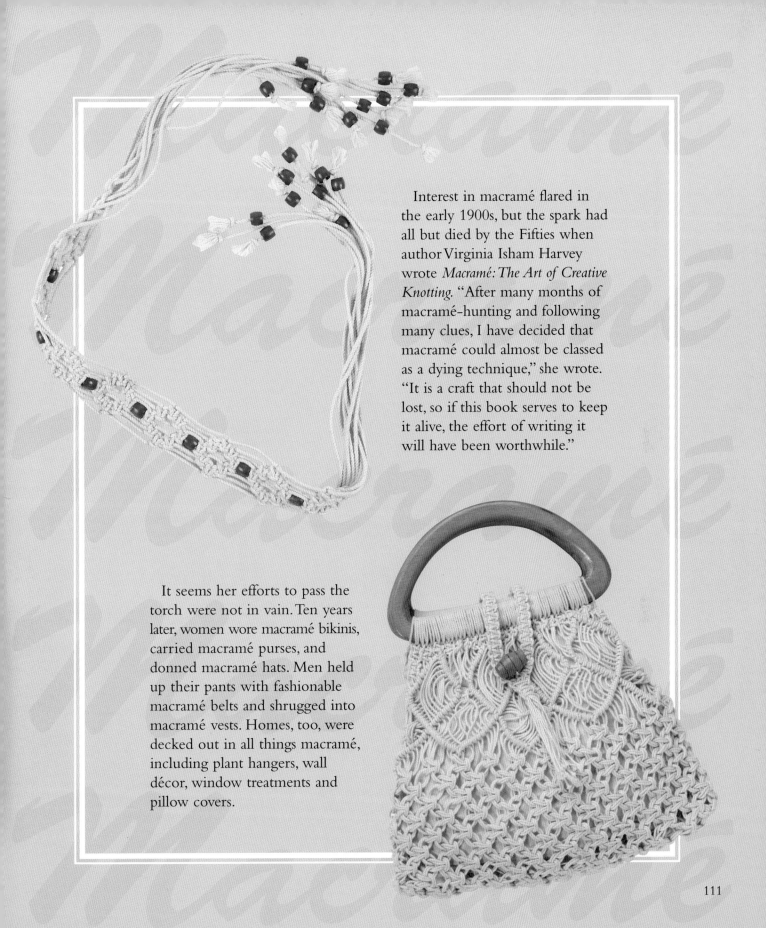

Interest in macramé flared in the early 1900s, but the spark had all but died by the Fifties when author Virginia Isham Harvey wrote *Macramé: The Art of Creative Knotting.* "After many months of macramé-hunting and following many clues, I have decided that macramé could almost be classed as a dying technique," she wrote. "It is a craft that should not be lost, so if this book serves to keep it alive, the effort of writing it will have been worthwhile."

It seems her efforts to pass the torch were not in vain. Ten years later, women wore macramé bikinis, carried macramé purses, and donned macramé hats. Men held up their pants with fashionable macramé belts and shrugged into macramé vests. Homes, too, were decked out in all things macramé, including plant hangers, wall décor, window treatments and pillow covers.

Let's do MACRAMÉ

The craft is inexpensive, simple and portable. All one needs for macramé are a few simple tools. Scissors to cut the cord, rubber bands to hold bundles of cord during project construction, and pins to hold the project to the work surface as necessary. As Harvey points out, some techniques require a base such as a foam-covered, fabric-wrapped board, a pillow weighted with a brick, or a stable post such as a doorknob, though other techniques require no base at all.

GLOSSARY OF MACRAMÉ TERMS

Anchor cords: Nonworking cords, such as the center cords in the square knot. Also known as "filler" cords.

Floaters: Unknotted cords.

Holding cord: An object onto which knotting cords are tied, such as another cord, dowel, purse handle, ring, or stick.

Knot bearer: The cord over which knots are tied.

Knotting cords: Cords used to tie the knots. Also known as "knotters."

Picots: Any number of small loops projecting beyond the work to form an ornamental edge.

Overhand knot: A looped knot that is tied with one or more cords.

It's EASY and FUN

"*It's really not that hard*"

Common Macramé Knots

Horizontal Half Hitch Bars with Double Half Hitches:

The half hitch is used to make bars. Bars are made over an end-working strand, called a "knot bearer." Always keep the knot bearer pulled taut. Form the knot with another working strand called the "knotting cord" over the knot bearer. Use pins to hold the knot bearer in place whenever necessary. With each working strand, make a half hitch as shown in Fig. 1A. Repeat, making a double half hitch as shown in Fig. 1B. Bars can be worked from right to left or from left to right (Fig. 1C).

Fig. 1A
Half Hitch

Fig. 1B
Double Half Hitch

Fig. 1C Horizontal Bar

Square Knot:

Made with four strands. Keep two center strands straight and tie knot with the two outer strands as shown in Figs. 2. Hold center strands taut and tighten knot by pulling the two outer strands up into place. A simple square knot may also be made with only two strands, eliminating the center strands.

Alternate Rows of Square Knots:

Make first row of square knots, using four strands for each. For second row, leave two strands at each side free and divide strands into groups of four, using two strands from adjacent knots of first row. Tie square knots across row, spacing row evenly below first row. For third row, use all strands as shown in Fig. 3 Repeat first row. Continue making each row wider than last. Decrease rows by leaving two more strands free on each side.

Diagonal and Double Diagonal Bars:

Made in same manner as Horizontal Half Hitch Bars with Double Half Hitches, but knot bearer is held diagonally downward to right or left as shown in Fig. 4. For double diagonal bars, use two end strands as knot bearers. Work double half hitches over outside strands for each bar, making second bar directly below first diagonal bar.

Vertical Double Half Hitch:

Use one working strand held vertically as shown in Fig. 5. Knot is made the same as for horizontal bar.

Alternate Half Hitches:

Work first double half hitch as for Fig. 5. Then, using second strand as knot bearer, make another double half hitch with first strand as shown in Fig. 6.

Reversed Double Half Hitch:

Make first half hitch by bringing working strand under knot bearer, around and over knot bearer, then under itself as shown in Fig. 7.

Overhand Knot:

A small knot is sometimes used to bring strands together as shown in Fig. 8A. Mounting cord also is knotted at both ends with an overhand knot as shown in Fig. 8B.

Sinnets:

Long lines made by repeating the first half of the square knot on four strands, which will twist the line as it grows. A variation of this is made by alternating double or vertical half hitches tied repeatedly around a knot bearer. To make a flat sinnet, repeat complete square knot on four strands.

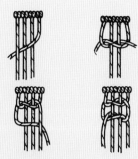

Fig. 2 Square Knots

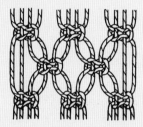

Fig. 3 Alternate Rows of Square Knots

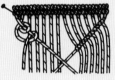

Fig. 4 Diagonal Bar – left and right

Fig. 5
Vertical Double
Half Hitches

Fig. 6
Alterante (double)
Half Hitches

Fig. 7
Reversed Double
Half Hitches

Fig. 8A
Overhand Knot

Fig. 8B Mounting

115

The only thing missing from this lovely garden room is . . . Macramé!

Simple Plant Hanger

The hanger is suspended from
a wood or metal ring, a great choice for larger plants.

Materials

- Plant pot
- Scissors
- Twine

Instructions

1. Measure from the center of the base of the pot to the height from which you intend to hang the pot, then add 12". Multiply this number by two, to determine the length of twine for this project.

2. If using medium–weight yarn, cut five lengths. If using a thicker rope, cut four lengths.

3. Gather one end of lengths together. Fold in half. Make an overhand knot approximately 4" from the fold. *Note: This is the top of the plant hanger.*

4. Place plant pot on work surface. Hold twine, or cord, next to pot to determine placement of first knot. The first knot should be at top rim of pot. Leave at least a few inches between top of hanger and first knot.

5. With two pieces of cord, make an overhand knot at top edge of the pot. Repeat with the remaining cords.

6. Arrange the knots so that they are equal distances from each other around the rim of the pot.

7. Hold two of the knots in place, choose one cord from each pair and pinch them together. This gives the position of the next row of knots.

8. Remove pot from cord basket.

9. Make an overhand knot where your fingers pinch the strands. Split remaining pairs of cords and make overhand knots at the same distance along the length of the cords.

10. Return the pot to the cord basket and repeat Steps 6–8.

11. Lay the basket around the outside of the pot. Using one cord from each of a pair of neighboring knots, measure to the bottom of the pot and pinch cords together. Hold these two cords together and remove pot from basket. With these same cords, make an overhand knot. *Note: The knot should come to bottom edge of pot.* Repeat with remaining cords. Return the pot to the basket and check the position of all knots.

12. Gather all ends of cord together to find best place for bottom of hanger. Mark this placement and remove pot from hanger. Tie an overhand knot with the gathered cords.

13. Trim the ends.

OUT OF AFRICA

GIRAFFE WALL HANGING

Based on a design by artist Susan Shwartz, our
giraffe would be equally at home in a living room,
game room, or even a child's room.

When the thought of making one more plant hanger, purse,
or belt no longer excites you, animal designs may offer just the distraction you need.
Instead of the cord and knots dictating the design, the design dictates the cord and knots.
Fun and creative, this project is easy enough for even the beginner to accomplish.

Materials

- 2 wooden beads, 1"
- 2 wooden beads, ½"
- 4 wooden beads, ¾"
- Brown 8-ply cord, 40 yds
- Gold 8-ply cord, 75 yds
- Macramé board
- Scissors
- Wire coat hanger
- Wire cutters

YARN FACTS
GIRAFFE
DETAILS

Use synthetic yarn for the giraffe project. Synthetic yarn is soft, flexible, and available in a wide variety of colors. Choose thick, twisted yarn; it unravels easily.

To create a furry look for the eyelashes and tail, unravel yarn by twisting it in the opposite direction from the way it is originally twisted. Separate individual plies. Brush unraveled yarn to achieve the effect of animal hair or fur. Use a wire brush for best results.

To make eye beads more lifelike, they can be stained a dark color or drawn on to create pupils and desired eye expressions.

Head

1. Stretch coat hanger into a diamond shape as shown in Fig. 1.
2. Cut twisted section and hook with wire cutters.

Horns and Forehead

1. Cut two 3-yard gold cords.
2. Tie an overhand knot in center of each cord
3. Fold each cord in half at knot.
4. Thread each end of folded cord through a 1" bead. Slide bead up to the knot.
5. Place one 1" bead at top of each wire horn.
6. Finish horns by tying square-knot sinnets of four knots each, using the wire as a filler and each pair of gold cords as tying cords.
7. To fill space between horns, crisscross the two middle cords, using one cord from each horn. *Note: The distance between horns should be 2" wide.*
8. Cut four 2½-yard brown cords.
9. Fold cords in half.
10. Attach one cord to each side of each horn, using a lark's head knot (a knot that leaves a cord on either side of a simple overhand knot).

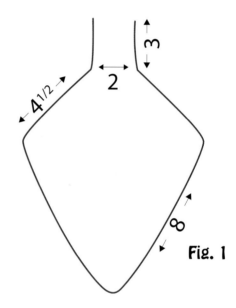

Fig. 1

Ears

1. Cut ten 3-yard gold cords, using five cords for each ear.
2. Tie an overhand knot in the center of two cords. Use one for each ear as an anchor cord.
3. Pin the anchor cords to board in an "A" shape with knots at top.
4. Attach to anchor chords with lark's head knots, then half-hitch with each of these cords.
5. Number all cords of each ear 1–10.
6. Using cord 5 as an anchor cord, tie a row of diagonal double half hitches with cords 4–2, working from inside to outside of ear.
7. Using cord 6 as an anchor cord, tie a row of diagonal double half hitches with cords 7–9, working from inside to outside of ear. Tie these directly below the row of knots tied in Step 4. Double-half-hitch right anchor cord around left anchor cord when center is reached.
8. Using same anchor cords, reverse direction and tie diagonal double half hitches, working down from

outside to inside of ear, forming a diamond shape.

9. Complete outer row (the outer bottom) of diamond, using anchor cords from Step 4. Tie diagonal double half hitches around these cords, working down from outside to inside. Double-half-hitch right anchor cord around left anchor cord when center is reached.

10. Tie cords 1 and 10 together on back of ear, then cut off excess cord. Repeat with cords 2 and 9.

11. With remaining six cords, tie two more rows of diagonal double half hitches, working from outsides to center. Double-half-hitch with right anchor cords around left anchor cords when center is reached.

12. Attach the six cords from each ear to outer corners of wire with double half hitches.

Face

1. Renumber all cords from ears and forehead 1–24. Gold cords will be 1, 2, 3, 4, 5, 6, 7, 10, 15, 18, 19, 20, 21, 22, 23, and 24. Brown cords will be 8, 9, 11, 12, 13, 14, 16, and 17.

2. Using cord 10 as anchor cord, work from center to left and tie double half hitches onto it with cords 9–1. Using cord 15 as anchor cord, work from center to right and tie double half hitches onto it with cords 16–24. Double-half-hitch anchor cords to wire. Tie them on back of head and cut off excess cord. Tie a second row of double half hitches directly under first row, using cords 11 and 12 as anchor cords. Repeat same steps for removal.

3. Renumber cords as in Step 1 of face. Slide one ¾" bead onto cords 2 and 3. Slide the remaining ¾" bead onto cords 18 and 19.

4. Beginning with cords 9–12, tie an alternating

square knot pattern that increases through the fifth row then decreases. Tie knots close together. Pick up additional cords on each side to increase rows. *Note: Reverse directions of knots on right half of face from those on left half.*

5. Slide one ½" bead onto cord 9 and one ½" bead onto cord 12. *Note: These are the nostrils.*

6. Tie two more decreasing rows of alternating square knots, ending with a row of one square knot.

7. Attach all cords to bottom of wire, using double half hitches. Tie cords together in back, and cut off excess.

8. To make eyelashes, attach two 8" scraps above each eye with lark's heads. Unravel cord and brush to fluff.

Neck

1. Cut two 6-yard gold cords and two 6-yard brown cords.

2. Fold each cord in half and attach to back of chin with lark's heads in this color order: gold, brown, brown, gold.

3. Tie 11 rows of alternating square knots, reversing the direction of knots on right half of neck from those on left half for proper coloration.

4. Cut two 6-yard gold cords and attach to outer scallops of row 10 with lark's heads.

5. Tie nine more rows of alternating square knots, as described in Step 3.

6. Cut two 6-yard gold cords and repeat Steps 4 and 5.

7. Tie a 27th row of square knots.

8. Tie a 28th row with only two alternating knots, centered, to taper neck.

9. Cut two 5-yard brown cords and attach to 28th row as in Step 4 of Face.

10. Using each of the four new brown cords as anchor

This doll isn't just for Suzy! Johnny will love the newest addition to his "zoo." And because this macramé giraffe is as durable as it is adorable, it withstands the test of time . . . and of Johnny. The sturdy head and neck are formed around a wire coat hanger. Frayed fibers make a fuzzy tail. Dark beads gleam just like Johnny's eyes. Go ahead, Johnny. Give it a hug!

cords, one per side per row, tie two "V" shaped rows of diagonal double half hitches, working from outsides to center. When center is reached, tie a double half hitch with left anchor cord around right anchor cord on each row.

11. Working from outside to center, tie a third row of double half hitches using the outermost gold cords as anchor cords. When center is reached, double-half-hitch left anchor cord around right anchor cord.

Legs

1. Renumber all cords 1–20.
2. Divide cords into four groups: 1–4, 5–10, 11–16, and 17–20.

Front legs

1. From groups 2 and 3 select the two shortest brown cords to use as fillers for a 26-knot square knot sinnet.
2. To make the sinnet, tie a square knot around the fillers with the two long brown cords. Then tie a square knot beneath the brown knot with the two gold cords.
3. Continue alternating colors, leaving brown tying cords in back and bringing gold tying cords to front to achieve the color effect shown in the photo. *Note: Each leg should have 26 knots, 13 of each color.*

Hind legs

1. Cut two 4-yard brown cords, one for each leg.
2. Fold each new brown cord in half and tie a square knot with it around the two shortest gold cords. You now have two brown tying cords, two gold tying cords and two gold filler cords.
3. Complete hind legs as you did in Steps 2 and 3 for the Front Legs.

Hooves

1. Cut excess filler cords below last square knot from legs.
2. Working from both sides to center, tie a "V" shaped row of double half hitches on each leg, using outermost cords on each leg as anchor cords. When centers are reached, tie a double half hitch around left anchor cords with right anchor cords.
3. Begin a second row of double half hitches, using new outer cords as anchor cords. After completing the first knot on each side of leg, attach a folded 21" brown scrap to each anchor cord and complete the row with other working cords. When center is reached, tie a double half hitch around right anchor cords with left anchor cords.
4. Tie the third and fourth rows with double half hitches, connecting each half in center with a double half hitch.
5. Trim excess cord ½" below last row of knots.

Tail

1. Tie one 24" gold scrap to back of neck.
2. Cut four 8" brown scraps and fold each in half.
3. Make a loop with the end of the gold cord. Leave 6" of gold cord showing between bottom of neck and loop.
4. Slip brown cords through loop and wrap all cords together where colors meet with a gathering knot, made with a separate gold scrap.
5. Unravel brown cords and brush.

How about some nice, warm
Acknowledgments

The inspiration for this book came from many sources – my grandmother's living room, Roundtop Texas, the retro ads of the '50s, '60s and '70s, and my own fond memories of my many crafting attempts from macramé, to latch hooking, to my favorite seashell shower curtain. I hope this walk down memory lane brings a smile to your face, as it did mine.

– **Jo Packham**

Bitchin' Editors:

Rebecca Ittner
Jenn Gibbs

Cool Cat Copyeditor:

Marilyn Goff

Kookie Book Designer:

Matt Shay

Groovy Cover Designer:

Matt Shay

Hip Photography and Styling:

Steve Aha
Anna Corba
Ryne Hazen
PussycatMagazine.com
Denise Trowbridge
Zac Williams

"Kitschy Crafts were instrumental in my upbringing and the development of my art and sense of style."

—Ron Davis

We would like to acknowledge the following companies, both past and present, whose fabulous vintage artwork, ads, designs, and photography provided a wonderful backdrop for our kitschy crafts.

Aldus Books London, Allis-Chalmers, American Gas Association, Avon, Beech Nut, Bon Ami Cleanser, Capehart Television, Career Club Shirts, Chen Yu Nail Lacquer, Chrysler, Clairol, Dodge, Dupont, Ficks-Reed, General Electric, Great Western Champagne, Hearst Publications, Hudson, IBM, International Harvester, Jantzen, Kelvinator, Leather Industries of America, Lehigh Cements, Magnavox Television, Miami Chamber of Commerce, Midol, Minnesota Woolens, Motorola, Nash, Nelson Doubleday, Orange Crush, Pacific Sheets, Penney's, Pyrex, Seagram's, Smirnoff, Spartan Radio, StrataLounger, Swans Down Cake Flour, Top Value Stamps, Trailer Coach Manufacturers Association, Volkswagen, Whitman's Chocolates, Worumbo Fabric

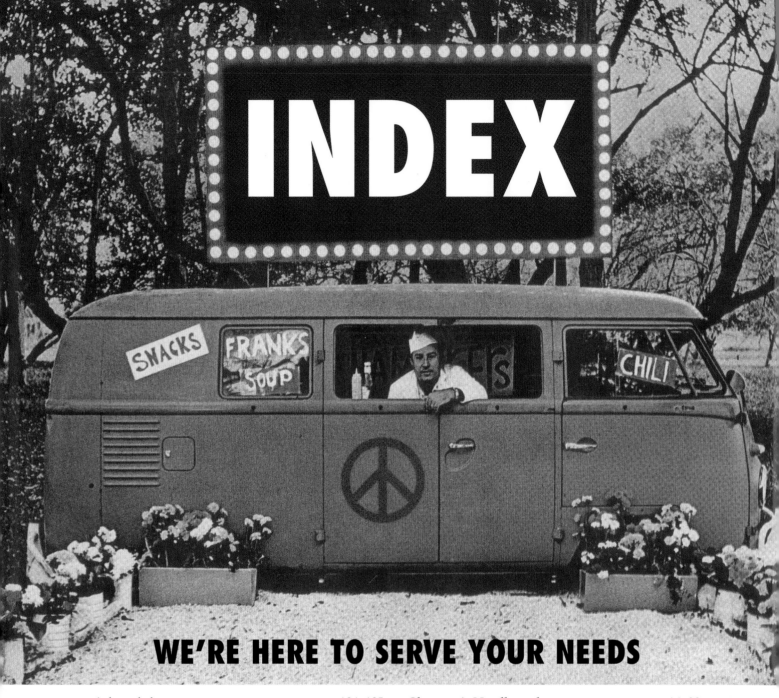

INDEX

WE'RE HERE TO SERVE YOUR NEEDS

Metric Conversion Chart

inches to millimeters and centimeters										yards to meters							
inches	mm	cm	inches	cm	inches	cm	yards	meters	yards	meters	yards	meters	yards	meters
⅛	3	0.3	9	22.9	30	76.2	⅛	0.11	2⅛	1.94	4⅛	3.77	6⅛	5.60
¼	6	0.6	10	25.4	31	78.7	⅛	0.11	2⅛	1.94	4⅛	3.77	6⅛	5.60
½	13	1.3	12	30.5	33	83.8	¼	0.23	2¼	2.06	4¼	3.89	6¼	5.72
⅝	16	1.6	13	33.0	34	86.4	⅜	0.34	2⅜	2.17	4⅜	4.00	6⅜	5.83
¾	19	1.9	14	35.6	35	88.9	½	0.46	2½	2.29	4½	4.11	6½	5.94
⅞	22	2.2	15	38.1	36	91.4	⅝	0.57	2⅝	2.40	4⅝	4.23	6⅝	6.06
1	25	2.5	16	40.6	37	94.0	¾	0.69	2¾	2.51	4¾	4.34	6¾	6.17
1¼	32	3.2	17	43.2	38	96.5	⅞	0.80	2⅞	2.63	4⅞	4.46	6⅞	6.29
1½	38	3.8	18	45.7	39	99.1	1	0.91	3	2.74	5	4.57	7	6.40
1¾	44	4.4	19	48.3	40	101.6	1¼	1.03	3¼	2.86	5⅛	4.69	7¼	6.52
2	51	5.1	20	50.8	41	104.1	1¼	1.14	3¼	2.97	5¼	4.80	7¼	6.63
2½	64	6.4	21	53.3	42	106.7	1⅜	1.26	3⅜	3.09	5⅜	4.91	7⅜	6.74
3	76	7.6	22	55.9	43	109.2	1½	1.37	3½	3.20	5½	5.03	7½	6.86
3½	89	8.9	23	58.4	44	111.8	1⅝	1.49	3⅝	3.31	5⅝	5.14	7⅝	6.97
4	102	10.2	24	61.0	45	114.3	1¾	1.60	3¾	3.43	5¾	5.26	7¾	7.09
4½	114	11.4	25	63.5	46	116.8	1⅞	1.71	3⅞	3.54	5⅞	5.37	7⅞	7.20
5	127	12.7	26	66.0	47	119.4	2	1.83	4	3.66	6	5.49	8	7.32
6	152	15.2	27	68.6	48	121.9								
7	178	17.8	28	71.1	49	124.5								
8	203	20.3	29	73.7	50	127.0								

See ya on the flipside.
Remember . . . keep it kitschy, keep it cool.

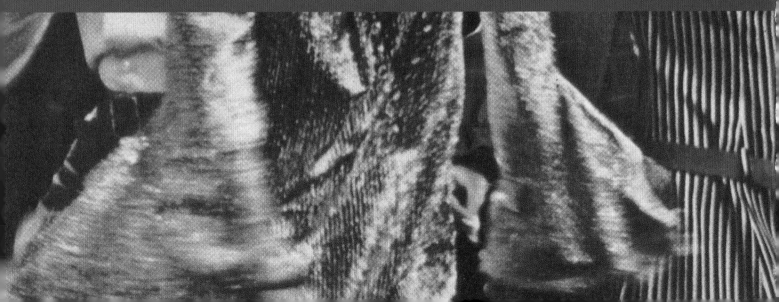